# Orchards

Practical orcharding for a changing planet

Andrew Lear and Margaret Lear

# Orchards

## Practical orcharding for a changing planet

THE CROWOOD PRESS

First published in 2023 by
The Crowood Press Ltd
Ramsbury, Marlborough
Wiltshire SN8 2HR

enquiries@crowood.com

**www.crowood.com**

**British Library Cataloguing-in-Publication Data**
A catalogue record for this book is available from the British Library.

ISBN 978 0 7198 4236 8

Typeset by Simon and Sons
Cover design by Sergey Tsvetkov
Printed and bound in India by Parksons Graphics Pvt Ltd

# Contents

# Planning Your Orchard

## I need space for an orchard ... don't I?

Fruit from your own orchard – what a wonderful thought! Freshly picked or stored for winter, no food miles, healthy and free from artificial chemical inputs – organic if you choose – a bountiful harvest to share with family and friends. But so many people shrink from the idea, thinking that they need masses of space, a field perhaps, or at least a large lawn dedicated to the fruit trees.

If you do happen to have a field begging to be converted to a standard commercial orchard, then the ideal trees exist for the purpose. But if you have nothing more than a balcony or patio, you can still plant a few fruit trees in pots and expect to get fruit from them. When an inventory of Scotland's orchards was undertaken in 2014, the criterion for being an orchard was having more than five fruit trees.[1] We counted up the ones we have secreted about our garden and got to forty very quickly! They do not need to be in a traditional orchard layout of rows. A surprising number can be accommodated along walls and fences and, if space is lacking, this need not be a problem as there are good dwarf trees available that are very productive.

In short, you can choose a tree that will fit nicely into any town garden and you can also find a grand, towering specimen befitting an old, traditional orchard. By the end of this book, we hope you will know just how to make the right choices for a successful orchard of any size.

Amazingly productive trees still survive in many old traditional orchards.

## Is my soil good enough?

Most fruit trees are marvellously adaptable and it's worth bearing in mind that many 'poor' soils are just soils that are trying to do better – and can be improved. Contaminated or poisoned ground would not be a good choice for your orchard, but by building deep, raised beds or investing in large planters, you can introduce soil and compost that will not harm your trees. Extremely acid soil (pH4 and under) is challenging, but fruit trees can grow in a wide range of acidity/alkalinity. Lime can be added to offset high acidity, although this needs to be done regularly. If you happen to live in the midst of acid 'peat bog', you might want to consider focusing on blueberries and cranberries, which like acidity – but remember that the planter/raised bed option is still there for apples and pears.

Dry, sandy soils, particularly on south-facing slopes, can be a source of drought stress for fruit trees and can also be less fertile. Be sure that you can get water to them easily, especially in spring. With climate change, droughts are something we must be increasingly aware of right across the country, although eastern parts and particularly the south-east of England are likely to be most affected. As for the lack of fertility, mulching with organic matter regularly and building fertility through green manures and other strategies can compensate for this (more on that in Chapter 4).

Don't worry too much if you have clay soil. Clay may be a nightmare to dig when dry and horribly sticky when wet, but it is also extremely fertile and holds water and nutrients for your trees to get at them. Some of the finest apple and pear orchards in Scotland in the nineteenth and early twentieth centuries were planted on the outrageously claggy clays of the Carse of Gowrie in Perthshire. Some are still thriving, despite seasonal waterlogging. But try to avoid putting your trees where water sits for extended periods. Snow melt that lies for a while but eventually drains is manageable, but if you see nothing but rushes, flag iris or other water-loving plants, avoid that spot. Fruit trees are adaptable, but they are not aquatic!

## Finding the best locations for your orchard trees

Trees will bear the best fruit if they have shelter from the wind, plenty of warmth and sunlight from March to October and enough water. This suggests that a south-west facing position is always better than a north-easterly one, as it will get more sunlight in early spring and late autumn. However, it could also frequently be in the teeth of prevailing westerly winds. In northern Europe, to get the best of both worlds, you will need to consider what shelter from the west your site already offers for an orchard and whether you can provide more in the form of shelter belts. Plant shelter belts of fast-growing trees at the same time as (or before) the orchard. Trees such as hazel and alder can be coppiced if they are getting too tall. Coppicing – cutting to the base – also encourages them to thicken up.

All houses have at least four walls. One or two will have a more or less southerly aspect and will be ideal for training fans or espaliers of pear trees, which blossom and ripen well with the reflected warmth and shelter. The house itself is a source of shelter, as are sheds, garages, fences, hedges and greenhouses. Tall shrubs and trees provide protection for an orchard. Conifers are particularly helpful, as their foliage usually runs right down to the ground, filtering out biting winds and slowing their speed. All evergreens provide year-round protection for early blossom, which is so prone to wind damage when the branches of deciduous shelter trees are bare. If you are shuddering at the thought of planting a Leylandii hedge – or simply don't have the space anyway – remember that sources of shelter in neighbouring properties are just as valuable. The wind knows no boundaries!

There are some situations where extreme measures might be taken to get a good crop from fruit trees. Fruit growers are nothing if not enterprising and

Use your walls to grow fruit trees.

determined. From the happily fruiting apple tree we've seen planted through the shelter of a vehemently tough rhododendron on the Atlantic coast of the Hebridean Isle of Lewis to dwarf cherry trees planted in polytunnels by commercial and amateur growers, there are solutions. Cherry trees are 100 per cent hardy, but so are blackbirds, which compete with the wind to keep humans and their cherries apart, hence the polytunnels. We also know apple orchards producing excellent crops in polytunnels on the Isle of Mull, whose citizens are not likely to let the odd blast of icy wind off the Atlantic get between them and their fruit! If you yearn for fruit that needs a little more warmth and sun than your climate presently provides, apricots and figs in the north will fruit better, earlier and sweeter if you incorporate them into a greenhouse or conservatory. You could even get lemons …

Thriving apple tree in Finstown, Orkney.

Fig trees, which thrive on warm, sunny walls.

Of course, too much shelter – or shelter that's too tall – will cut off essential light and warmth. There has to be a trade-off and every situation will demand a different compromise. A garden at sea level on a western coast, or a farm orchard at 250m (820ft) altitude in hill country, will need lots of shelter to thrive, so some sunlight will have to be sacrificed. An orchard at the head of a deep, south-facing valley, or a garden in a woodland glade, may be fine for shelter, but sites for trees will need to be selected for maximum sunlight.

## The risks to orchard trees from the weather

From the preceding comments about shelter, you will have guessed that windy weather can be detrimental to successful fruit growing. There are several ways in which the orchard is affected by wind:

- Strong winds between March and May can literally rip the blossom from trees – no blossom, no fruit.
- Bees and early pollinators won't be able to fly in strong winds, reducing the numbers of fruit formed.
- In August and September, wind can tear leaves to shreds, break branches and blow unripe fruit off the tree.

However, wind – and cold temperatures – in winter rarely do much damage, as the trees are dormant and not in leaf, so there is little wind resistance. Snow lying for any length of time has no direct effect, but beware of the voles sheltering cosily under the snow and spending the winter munching through the bark and shallow roots at the foot of each tree. Also a risk are rabbits using heavy snowfalls to reach above the rabbit guard you thought was protecting your trees, for a meal of the bark above it.

Frost is a perennial problem in most parts of the British Isles. None of our commonly-grown orchard trees will succumb to it themselves – but blossom can. Frosts up until mid-April can kill the exposed blossom of early flowering trees such as cherry-plum and pear, with early apples also at risk. Curiously, if the blossom escapes and the fruit is well set, it is less susceptible, although late frosts can damage embryonic fruitlets and newly unfurling leaves in April. There are some more frost-hardy varieties reputed to give reliable crops on cold sites; for example, Keswick Codlin apples. However, the problem can't be avoided by only planting late-flowering varieties of apple, as late frosts can still play havoc right through May in many areas and in some years. This is one very good reason for planting a mixed orchard – something we will return to. At least then you will get a crop of something every year.

Summer brings fewer challenges to fruit growers from the weather. Indeed, warmth brings fruit

Cherry-plum in flower, 18 March.

considered very welcome by orchard owners, there are cases where intensely hot sun has caused the bark on exposed trees to split and fruit literally to get sunburn – a warning not to prune away protective foliage too harshly in summer.

## What about the changing climate?

Yes, our climate is changing and we are seeing long-term trends that are still hard to predict. Apples appear to be flowering some fourteen days earlier than they did forty years ago, providing more evidence of climate warming. Warmer summers may be good for producing better fruit in the north of Scotland, but bad news if you're in the south of France – or England – where droughts are becoming the norm.

Climate warming on a global scale brings changes in air currents that also usher in more rain and more floods – and great uncertainty. The kinds of fruit we can grow may change, making experimentation on a small scale worthwhile, but there are no certainties. It will become increasingly hard to protect your fruit trees, as you simply will not be able to judge what will be thrown at them next by weather extremes. This is another reason not to put all your eggs in one basket; it is best to grow a range of species and a range of varieties of each major type, and to grow them in different ways.

on nicely, but extreme weather such as a late summer hailstorm can still damage ripening fruit. In mainland Europe, commercial growers put up enormous nets over trees to protect the crop from hailstones. And although heat and sunshine are usually

This wind-damaged pear is still alive!

## Orchard styles

Just as there is no set size for an orchard, there is no correct way to organise the trees and the layout should reflect your personal tastes, convictions and the features of the space chosen. Here we look at some of the more obvious styles, all of which can be adapted to suit your site.

### The traditional orchard

If you have a very large lawn (more than 100sq m [1,076sq ft]) or expanse of grass and do not incline towards endless mowing and neat, green stripes, planting fruit trees in traditional rows (running north to south for maximum sunlight) might be your answer. The advantage of rows is that it's easier to carry out essential grass cutting with machinery than informal spacing, though there's no necessity for straight lines if you can manage the space in-between.

In old orchards, 5m (16ft) spacing was the norm, separating tall, spreading standard trees on vigorous rootstocks. As gardeners retired, or were lost for war, pruning tended to be neglected. This became an issue with such large trees and much fruit would never be picked. Traditional towering trees came to be seen as wasteful. It is perfectly possible, however, to adopt a traditional style, but use trees on less

vigorous rootstocks to overcome these problems. Crucially, a wide mix of species and varieties can be planted, including local heritage trees. This makes the style ideal for community orchards. Make sure that the names of the trees don't get lost – if it's a public space, clear labels and information add value and create interest.

Whatever the rootstock, free-standing trees will still need to be 3–5m (10–16ft) apart from each other, so calculate the number of trees you can fit in by drawing a rough plan. Plums and damsons tend to be taller and grow more vigorously than apples and pears, so avoid planting them at the south end and shading out the latter. Plums and damsons are also more at ease growing in part-shade than apples and (especially) pears. Damsons under taller trees, or planted in a hedge, can still produce well.

The traditional orchard will later give you lots of options for maintaining the sward of grass underneath. Try not to design for strimmers! For starters, it does not have to be just grass. Gooseberries, strawberries and other soft fruit have been grown in alleys under orchard trees successfully in many areas, such as Scotland's famous Clyde Valley Orchards, which have seen quite a revival in recent years. Design the width of the alley to suit the crop and to facilitate easy weed control.

Chickens can also be kept in the orchard, once the trees are well established enough for the roots not to

Informal orchard.

be scratched to pieces, but ducks and geese are far better grazers if you want to cut down on mowing. Sheep in the orchard look romantic, but *please* box in the trees to keep them really well protected. We are convinced that lambs can pass through the eye of a needle if there's an apple tree to browse on the other side of it. Also, remember that the reason the pig-gy-wig in the wood had a ring through the end of his nose, his nose, was to stop him digging up the trees ...

## The walled garden

The traditional Scottish walled garden – also found in the rest of Britain – was designed and sited to grow phenomenal crops, avoiding the forays of farm and wild animals, as well as occasionally brutal and punishing weather hazards. Considering the outside and inside of the garden, there are eight wall borders, two each of north-, east-, south- and west-facing. Four are in a protective enclosure, four open to the elements but with walls behind them. If you can replicate this on any scale, you will have dazzling opportunities!

Traditionally, the shadier outside walls would be occupied by nursery beds of young plants and trees, but those walls getting good sunlight would also be planted with fans, espaliers and cordons of suitable fruit trees. Remember, a wall not only shelters and supports the tree planted against it, but also reflects the warmth and sunlight it receives. Inside the walled garden, a microclimate is created by shelter and reflected heat, making for remarkable possibilities. North-facing walls are shady for a good part of the day, but the soil stays moist and these conditions suit the acid 'cooking' cherries such as Morello and the shade-tolerant black, red and whitecurrants. Damsons are content on a north wall, too, but will produce better fruit on east- and west-facing walls, which will receive most of their sunlight either in the morning or afternoon, thus providing plenty of ripening time. West-facing walls suit most apples, plums and green-gages, but be aware that, even in an enclosed garden, they may also get more wind. East walls tend to be colder, but early-fruiting apples, plums and cherries, as well as soft fruit, can be trained against them.

South-facing walls? Everything mentioned above will thrive – but be aware that the soil against south walls dries out in hot weather and cherries will hate this. Pear trees love being against a south-facing wall. Traditional walled gardens often had part of the south wall occupied by glasshouses, in which vines and more tender fruit would be grown. It's common in Scotland to see chimneys poking incongruously from the wall (which was hollow). A boiler heated the spaces between the inner and outer wall, creating yet more warmth for peaches, nectarines and apricots to flower without risk from frost and to encourage fruit to ripen early out of doors. In the south-east corner,

Sheep eat fruit trees, so be warned!

Fruit trees can be grown to a fan shape on walls.

Trees grown closely together as cordons against a wall.

basking in sun and shelter, there would be fig trees. You don't necessarily need the boiler and hollow wall, by the way – we know of peach trees in Scotland still fruiting regularly in walled gardens where the fires have long been extinguished.

So, a mini-walled garden may be for you – or, perhaps, a community can take on and restore a derelict one. It's been done....

## The forest garden orchard

Permaculture, forest gardening, or food forests are alternative ways to envisage your orchard. These are definitely options if you have limited space but want to harvest maximum food from your garden. They are a way forward, also, for larger-scale, community-led initiatives in public open spaces. Fruit (and nut) trees are grown as the forest canopy species in an area or bed that also contains food-producing shrubs such as berries and currants, nitrogen-fixing and soil-improving shrubs (preferably with an edible or other use), plants for pollinators and wildlife, plus a range of herbs and edible perennial plants as the ground layer. The fruit trees will, of course, provide shade. In a small plot, this might be too much, but can be remedied by using dwarfing rootstocks and training the trees as cordons or stepovers on the perimeter.

A forest garden should be allowed to develop organically, especially with regard to ground layer and low shrubs, and how it's maintained will be suggested by what is happening naturally. For example, mint in the ground layer might become too dominant and need controlling, or an optimistic inclusion of an olive tree might fizzle out and be replaced by a tougher berry. It's a different way to grow food. It can all go pear-shaped (one hopes!), but it can also be amazingly productive and is excellent news for biodiversity and the planet.

One popular variation on the forest garden that can be incorporated into many domestic gardens and works brilliantly in community projects is the 'edible fruiting hedge', mixing native shrubs with 'top fruit' (orchard trees) and 'soft fruit' (shrubs bearing berries and currants), nuts and climbers. It is a good way of making use of the vertical space in restricted areas.

## The patio orchard

There's no such thing as a dwarf fruit tree … *but* you can buy a fruit tree of most types on a very dwarfing rootstock that will give you a miniature tree and plenty of fruit if planted in a large enough container (minimum 20ltr [4.5gal]). We'll tell you more about rootstocks and the ones to get for the patio orchard

Upright cordons are productive, do not cast much shade and take up little space.

Edible hedges need to be allowed to grow to produce fruit.

in Chapter 3. If you have paving laid on sand over soil, consider lifting one or two slabs and planting a fruit tree in the gap. Think about the space-saving ways of training fruit trees as cordons or stepovers (described in Chapter 5). You could probably fit three cordon apples against a balcony. One advantage of the patio orchard is that tender varieties can be moved about or indoors if bad weather is forecast – and of course you have flexibility to change things around. There are also usually handy areas of wall on which to capitalise!

## The commercial orchard

If your proposed orchard is going to work in a commercial sense, easy maintenance is essential. Planting in straight rows is a good start, as is making the rows the right width apart for the minimum number of passes of whatever you will be using to mow or maintain the orchard. Do not forget to allow for a turning circle at the end of each row. The closer the spacing is between trees in the rows, the easier it will be to cut weed competition. This is usually achieved by chemical control in the commercial world, but it doesn't have to be and isn't in our fruit gardens – weed-suppressant ground matting and mulching will also do the job. Wildflower verges to the orchard will help to attract pollinators.

You can only have the trees very close if you use a dwarfing or very dwarfing rootstock (*see* Chapter 3). Harvesting the crop will also be easier from dwarf trees – no climbing! The fruit can be picked from ground level. Such dwarf trees will need support from tall posts all their life, but they are otherwise easy to maintain and prune, trimming wayward branches back to within the rows. The methods used by professionals to keep these trees producing well is described in Chapter 5. Typically, fewer varieties will be grown, being focused on what will sell and keep, or for specific purposes such as cider-making. In the latter case, however, do not be too concerned about dwarfing rootstocks. Height does not matter, as cider apples, when grown commercially, are shaken from the trees.

Apples and pears can do very well in a half-barrel.

## Community orchards, linear orchards and biodiversity

We would suggest strongly that whatever type of orchard you plan, it is made as biodiverse as possible. You need insect pollinators if you're going to get any fruit at all. You also need predators, especially invertebrates and birds, in order to maintain a healthy balance of wildlife. The non-biodiverse orchard is the one where all the pests and diseases hang out and chemical sprays creep in. Old, traditional orchards are one of the best habitats for wildlife in Britain, so in planning your orchard, think not only of what it can give you, now, but what it could become for nature in future decades or centuries.

It stands to reason that the bigger the orchard, the greater its potential for providing habitats for invertebrates, birds, herpetofauna and mammals, together with other plant species, fungi, lichens and

Trees are planted very close together in modern orchards.

microfauna. If a community can come together and buy, beg or appropriate a parcel of unused land, there are benefits not just to biodiversity, but in terms of shared labour, harvest and variety on a scale that a single family may not achieve in their back garden. Some councils are happy for community organisations to take on the management of a public open space. They and private landowners may be amenable to adapting a roadside verge to become a productive linear orchard, for all visitors to help themselves to fruit in the autumn. Good examples, local to us, are the Gas Brae Linear Orchard in Errol, in the middle of the Carse of Gowrie historic orchard area of Perthshire, and the Dunkeld & Birnam Community Orchard – a large orchard and soft-fruit garden planted fifteen years ago beside the River Tay and thriving.

Fruit trees themselves attract a wide range of wildlife, of course, both through blossom and fruit. Long grass between tree rows and uncut verges with wildflowers should feature, but also areas of short grass where fungi can flourish and owls can successfully hunt those pesky voles. There's lots more ideas on all this in Chapters 6 and 12.

So, you do have the space. Your soil is good enough, or can be made so. The weather is beyond your control, but can be planned for. You've chosen what type of orchard suits you best. Now it's time to choose the trees!

Old trees can develop a hollow trunk.

# An apple mythology

The word 'paradise' actually comes from a Persian term meaning orchard and a symbiosis arose between the fruits of the orchard and the idea of heaven or paradise. In ancient Greece, there was a special emphasis on apple trees and apples. Apples were believed to confer immortality on those who received and ate them – that is, apples from a certain sacred tree, at least.

In the Greek pantheon, the ruler of the gods was Zeus and his queen was Hera. But before these two upstarts there was Gaia. Gaia was the mother of all the gods and the mother of all – Mother Earth, if you like. When Zeus married Hera, Gaia's gift to her daughter-in-law was the sacred apple tree that bore such powerful fruit. It was planted in the magical Orchard, or Garden, of the Hesperides in paradise. And who were the Hesperides? A band of nine maidens, who were minor love goddesses tasked with care of the orchard and serving as guardians of the sacred apple tree. Like all orchardists, the Hesperides were inveterate scrumpers, or stealers, of apples, and the sacred tree never seemed to get its full number of fruit to ripen. Hera got a bit cross about this and put a giant serpent-like dragon called Ladon into the orchard to guard the sacred tree and its fruit. Ladon curled up in the roots and got to work.

Enter the labours of Heracles, the eleventh of which was to steal three golden apples from the sacred tree. With a good deal of trickery and under-handed dealings, he succeeded. But his success included, sadly, the death of Ladon, the guardian serpent. Angry Hera set Ladon into the sky as a star constellation: the one we know as Draco, the Dragon. Heracles benefited nothing from his labour and was obliged to return the three apples to the Hesperides.

Fast-forward to the early Middle Ages in Britain. The same motifs surround the Isle of Avalon, a magical place for healing and the meeting of mythologies. Avalon means Apple Orchard. It is widely taken to refer to an area that is now dry marshland in the Somerset Levels, which when sea levels were higher would have made the high ground known today as Glastonbury Tor an island. So many tales meet together in that area, from Arthurian to New Age, but one story was that the apples from the trees there conferred not immortality, but the gift of prophecy, and they were guarded and tended not by minor love goddesses (although there is certainly a dragon implicated at the Tor), but the people of Faerie. In the thirteenth century, a Scot named Thomas is said to have met the Queen of Faerie, received some magic apples and became a famous seer, known as Thomas the Rhymer.

## Chapter Two

# Choose Your Trees

There are a number of important things you need to think about when deciding what trees to plant in your orchard:

- What species of fruit trees to include.
- What varieties to choose and their suitability for your location.
- What nursery availability there is of your chosen trees.
- How much of each fruit you want to produce and what you plan to do with it.
- How big you want the trees to grow and if/how you plan to train them.
- How to ensure that there are pollinisers – trees that will cross-pollinate – in the vicinity.

Let's look at each consideration in turn.

## A wide range of possibilities

### Pip fruit

Most orchardists will want apples to be included in the mix. They are the easiest of the tree fruits to grow and perfect for a beginner to start with. There are apples that will grow everywhere in Britain from Sussex to Stornoway, from Lerwick (with a bit of help) to Land's End. Most of the apples we eat nowadays have a long history of breeding and selection from the wild apples of Kazakhstan or China and bear little resemblance to the sour, wild crabs sometimes found in British woodlands. These selected fruits were gradually introduced into Europe over the centuries. You can still find the Pomme d'Api, believed to have been in cultivation since Roman times, and all our modern varieties have been produced from older selections.

A limited number of varieties are available in garden centres.

The Roman apple, Pomme d'Api.

Pears are almost as popular as apples and hardier than people think. They are also extremely long-lived as fruit trees, with a long and fascinating history as part of the diet of these islands. The 'crab' form of wild pear is called – tellingly – a choker. Since earliest times, the range and types of pears in Britain have been local, eclectic and changeable, many home-bred, but from early European scions.

## Stone fruit

The wild cherry, or gean, is a mighty tree when grown, too big for most gardens. It bears fabulous blossom, as well as edible fruit that are variable in colour, size and sweetness. They are often more white than red. Old photographs show the very tall ladders needed to harvest these fruit. Modern, cultivated cherries have been bred and selected all around the world, especially Canada. On dwarfing rootstocks, they are easier to pick (no ladders or aptly named 'cherry pickers') and to keep protected from the large number of birds and other cherry gourmands who compete with the orchard owner for a taste.

Plums, damsons and gages are the other orchard mainstays, with plums probably being most people's 'must-have'. They have their origins in several wild species of *Prunus*, but not species native to Britain. Bullace (*Prunus insititia*) and sloe (*Prunus spinosa*) are our natives, the fruit of which bears no resemblance to the large, luscious garden plum, but any 'wild' plums found growing are probably descended from garden escapes. The National Fruit Collection at Brogdale in Kent holds a wide range of plums – sweet, acid, intense, aromatic, marble-sized to monstrous and any colour from greenish-yellow to darkest purple – but, for various reasons, surprisingly few make it into the garden. It's hard not to want them all!

Damsons were once named Damascenes. They take their name from Damascus in Syria, where they have been cultivated for millennia. In Westmorland, north-west England, the damsons are propagated by root suckers, which makes them clones of

Old pear trees can be an important landscape feature.

Having said that, sometimes apples on trees sprouted from pips discarded from a railway carriage can be rather good! Now and then, a new apple is 'discovered' in this way.

Blue, yellow and black plums are relatively unknown in gardens.

Mirabelles (cherry-plums) are hardy and easy to grow.

introductions made many centuries ago! The small, musky, purple fruit are valued in preserve-making, but are very difficult to resist straight from the tree. If you have an awkward or shady spot, plant a damson there and it will probably thrive.

Gages, which originated in Iran, are not always green, but they are always of a choice flavour and much sought after. They are perceived as being more difficult than plums and damsons, partly because some are unable to self-pollinate. This is not true of them all, however, and if you have room for a gage or two, you will be the envy of the neighbourhood. Greengages are the sweetest of fruits and hide in amongst the foliage. Some gardeners are not aware of the bounty lurking above their heads!

Mirabelles, or cherry-plums, are also stone fruit, just like plums, but resemble large cherries in shape and size. The fruit can be red or yellow or anything in-between, but are always sweet and very moreish.

They are widely grown as smaller orchard trees in mainland Europe, especially France, and some choice cultivars can be obtained. The best known is probably the Mirabelle de Nancy. Here, you will sometimes come across cherry-plums in very old orchards, where they were once used as a rootstock on which to graft plums. Over the centuries, the plum trees have died, but the cherry-plum rootstock has taken over, sometimes providing a more plentiful crop than the plum did and should definitely be more widely appreciated. They can also be planted as part of a hedging scheme or as garden ornamentals, for they flower profusely very early in the year. Then in late July, one will find find pavements and lawns littered with delicious little fruit that their owners have disregarded, unaware of their edibility. They are tough little trees that thrive in challenging conditions, but, sadly, in hedges most of the fruiting wood is hacked away in the annual 'prune'.

## Unusual fruits

Apart from the mainstream orchard trees, you may have just the spot for something unusual:

### Peaches and nectarines
Nothing can beat a peach or nectarine from your own tree, but in much of Britain, you really need an unheated greenhouse or some protection from frost, which can destroy the very early flowers. The warmth and shelter of an open glasshouse can also help the fruit to sweeten and ripen. In milder areas, a south-facing wall will provide the right conditions. Easy to grow, prolific and self-fertile, we swear our peaches are superior to anything you'll buy in the supermarket.

### Apricots
As with peaches, some protection or a warm, sheltered spot will provide the right conditions for apricots. A word of warning: sometimes you may see apricot trees growing outside and setting fruit. These may be ornamental cultivars, which have high concentrations of cyanides in the stones and are not for eating.

### Medlars
Perhaps the most unusual of our top fruits, the medlar bears large, single white flowers that form strange-looking, hard brown fruit within the flower calyx. They are not edible until they have 'bletted' – a polite way of saying started to rot – when they become soft, sweet and have a lovely smell. Really! Eat from the shell with a teaspoon, or make into delicious medlar jelly.

### Quinces
In a sunny, protected corner, the tree quince (*Cydonia oblonga*), which is distinct from the (equally edible) shrub known as the Japonica

A basket of medlars – ripe when rotting!

quince, will yield large, yellow, lumpy, fuzzy fruit with a strong flavour and a peculiar, sweet perfume. It rarely gets sweet enough here to eat raw, but apple pies with quince in them are out of this world. It is an untidy tree, but we've spotted it trained as an espalier, which is much neater and hopefully as productive.

### Mulberries
Mulberries tend to be a feature of old cathedral squares and gardens, where shelter and the heat reflected from paving really suit this spreading tree. It has weeping foliage and choice, raspberry-like fruit that need the warmth of walls and buildings to become their sweet and juicy best.

### Figs
Once again, a warm wall (south-west facing is ideal, or a corner) or cold greenhouse will be the best site for this tree to produce its delicious Mediterranean fruit. It's surprisingly easy to grow given its region of origin and even a young plant in a pot will do well. Overwintering large fruit sadly tend to drop off; it's the spring-formed figs that ripen over the summer. Tradition says to plant a fig tree in a box or surrounded by slabs, in order to restrain the roots and stop them taking energy from fruit production.

## Nuts

There are several good varieties of cobnut related to our native hazel (*Corylus avellana*), which would happily grow to 30m (100ft) if given the freedom to do so. Usually, they are coppiced to keep them small and easily harvested. Be warned – they also have a vigorous root system, so get the right spot first time! Filberts, cultivars of *Corylus maxima*, differ by having a larger sheath around the nut, but are otherwise similar. The purple-leaved cultivar is especially attractive, with long, purple catkins. We recommend planting a few different varieties to help with cross-pollination. Other nut trees to consider include walnuts, if you have space. Modern cultivars start producing prolifically while still young.

## Right place, right variety?

The choice in most garden centres, unfortunately, is usually limited to a few English or Europe-bred varieties. Most of us have only the rather limited range found on supermarket shelves to guide us – but remember, these have usually been imported from different, usually warmer, climates. Even if you can get the same variety, you may find that they don't taste the same when grown in your personal corner of the British Isles and, as only the visually perfect have been selected for supermarket use, you are tasting a very biased sample. There are many varieties that originated here and were selected for our local climates that will taste every bit as good – better, perhaps – than the supermarket imports.

The most important advice we can give you when choosing varieties is: look local. What are the best apples in your neighbours' gardens? What varieties does your nearest specialist nursery recommend for your situation? Ask, question, taste, reflect; for example, what texture and flavour are you looking for?

Consider apples. There are so many varieties of apple tree on the market, it will be difficult to decide which to include. Every region has its own heritage varieties and its own great performers. If you live in Morayshire, how can you not grow the apple Beauty of Moray, or neglect Stirling Castle apple despite its lack of vigour, if your orchard is under the shadow of that great fortification? We have specialised in reviving Scottish varieties (of which there are still over forty apples alone in existence), but look local, wherever you are. Cider apples from Herefordshire, the Norfolk Beefing from East Anglia, Keswick Codlin from the Lakes, Beauty of Bath, Worcester Pearmain, the Bardsey Apple from Wales ... the list goes on and on. And that's just apples! Add in Pershore plums, Westmorland damsons, Hessle or Hazel pears from Hull, perry pears and the Black Pear of Worcester and many more. You may be lucky and find your region has a local 'Pomona' or list of apple or other fruit varieties grown there.

Heritage and local varieties, of course, are not the only options and many may be hard to obtain commercially (which is where acquiring grafting skills may be a good idea – *see* Chapter 3). It would be foolish to ignore the many, very choice modern varieties that are on the market, bred in many countries and climates. We would suggest that you look at varieties grown and selected in parts of the world with a similar climate to yours. For example, we have always taken an interest in Scandinavian varieties for growing in western Scotland and most have done very well. They may also have advantages in genetic traits such as

Westmorland damson.

## Rosemoor Devon heritage apple collection

**Eaters**

A D W Atkins
Bradninch Black (Devon Pendragon)
Devon Crimson Queen
Greasy Butcher
Hollow Core (Glasbury)
Johnny Voun
Listener (Lucombe's seedling, Crediton Fair &
    Kirton fair)
Pigs Nose 3
Plum Vitae (Venus Pippin, Plumderity)
Queens
Sugar Bush
Sweet Cleave
Twenty Pip
Veitches Perfection

**Cookers**

Don's Delight
Endsleigh Beauty
Grand Sultan (Cornish Pine, Red Ribbed Greening)
Limberlimb
No Pip
Payhembury
Poltimore Seedling
Quarry
Reverend McCormick
Stockbearer
Summer Stubbard (Summer Stibbert, S Queeing)
Totnes Apple (dual, keeper)
Winter Stubbard

**Ciders**

Blue Sweet

Court Royal
(Sweet Blenheim, Pound)

Billy Down Pippin

Crimson Victoria

Dufflin

Goring

Hangy Down
(Pocket Apple)

Johnny Andrews

Kingston Bitter

Netherton Late Blower
(Town Farm 59)

Paignton Marigold

Royal Wilding (Cadbury)

Spotted Dick

Sweet Bay

An extraordinary number of Devon apples can be seen at RHS Garden Rosemoor.

disease resistance or precocious fruiting. One good example of this is the apple Katy – also known as Katja – from Sweden, one of our most popular eating apples. If you are nearer the south coast of Britain, you may do well with some of the fantastic French varieties, like the many apples in the Reinette group, or luscious pears like the Jargonelle (which actually does well in Perthshire too, if not quite as reliably as the local pear, Craig's Favourite).

In this book, we have listed many varieties for varying purposes, such as disease resistance, pollination needs or storage potential. We can't give you a list of 'the best' varieties of apple, pear or plum, because taste is subjective and every orchardist has different priorities and quirks when selecting the trees they want to grow. It would be impossible to list every variety available to you, unhelpful not to describe each one and unfair to leave any out. So, here is our personal Top 20 (Table 1) – but as you can see, we don't even agree with each other and have had to make two lists!

The 'sausage pear'.

# Table 1: Authors' favourite varieties of fruit

| Andrew's top ten | Margaret's top ten |
|---|---|
| **Apple George Cave**<br>because it's early, a prolific producer and crisp (according to Andrew) | **Apple White Melrose**<br>for the big, round, easy-peel, pure white fleshed fruit that froth delightfully if cooked, are tasty raw and for its history |
| **Apple Quinte**<br>because of its odd oval shape, deep maroon skin and white, fizzy flesh | **Greengage Cambridge Favourite**<br>because it is mouth-wateringly juicy and sweet and is eaten straight off the tree |
| **Apple Discovery**<br>because of its lovely aroma; a bright red, round, 'apply' apple | **The 'sausage pear'**<br>which grows in a neglected Perth orchard and has crisp, juicy, misshapen fruit and no name; DNA tests mark it as unique (Margaret loves a good mystery) |
| **Apple St Edmund's Russet**<br>because it is gloriously flavoured in a good season (and is the apple that converted Andrew to russets) | **Apple Cox Pomona**<br>which is sharp and juicy in a good year (and reminds Margaret of a much-loved neighbour and his orchard, where she first bit into one) |
| **Pear Longueville (aka the Rattray pear)**<br>because of its solid juiciness and lovely spotty green and brown skin | **Apple Discovery**<br>because it's sweet and alluring (and was the main tree in the neighbour's orchard) |
| **Cherry-plums**<br>for the lovely surprise of finding them falling out of hedgerows and over garden walls in late July | **Apple Lord Derby**<br>because it's a great cooker and waits politely on the tree till last, without hassling to be processed |
| **Greengage Cambridge Favourite**<br>because they hide away in people's gardens and the owners may be unaware of the very sweet, gorgeous little fruit | **Apple Bloody Ploughman**<br>because it's local, very refreshing and juicy; an unmistakable dark red, with a great backstory |
| **Apple Red James Grieve**<br>because it's a sweet, crisp eater (to begin with), but won't keep and is less susceptible to scab than green forms of James Grieve | **Pear Craig's Favourite**<br>because it's nearly as good as the 'sausage pear', doesn't dribble down the chin and is sublime poached in red wine |
| **Damson Shropshire Prune**<br>because of its tasty late fruit hanging in pendulous branches | **Cherry-plum Mirabelle de Nancy**<br>because there are so many things you can do with it, including eat the lot as you pick them |
| **Apple Galloway Pippin**<br>because it makes a vigorous, robust tree bearing solid, round cookers (also its close relation, the eater Siddington Russet) | **Apple Hawthornden**<br>because it's prolific, reliable and cooks extremely well; also a good addition to cider |

## A Matter of Taste

Whether you choose heritage or modern, local or well-travelled settlers, it's important that most of the fruit in your orchard is fruit you enjoy eating and can use. We disagree on what is a nice apple. Andrew likes his apples soft, spongy, sweet and with thin skins. Margaret likes apples with bite, crunch and a sharpness to offset the sweet. In our orchard, you will find both, alongside plenty we just *have* to have for the name, the story behind them, or the place they come from.

One thing we puzzle over is the British determination to divide top fruit into dessert or culinary varieties. In particular, what is a 'cooking' plum? We have never come across a plum or damson that isn't delicious straight from the bush, or that requires cooking to soften it and sugar to make it palatable. There are, admittedly, some pears (such as Black Worcester and several ancient Scottish varieties) that need to be cooked, or might even be best treated as savoury vegetables, and the 'sour' cherries are the best ones for pies. With everything else, it's quite honestly a matter of taste. A lot of Scottish apples are listed automatically as cookers; we find many of these delectable eaten fresh. James Grieve is routinely described as 'dual purpose', but we would only ever cook them if there were too many and we needed to preserve the harvest.

In mainland Europe, distinctions are not made between cooking and eating apples, and there is really, truly, no reason (beyond the sensitivities of digestion) why you can't eat a cooking apple raw, or cook a sweet dessert apple. Look, rather, at what happens to the flesh when the apple is cooked. For some desserts, you will want the apple to become a froth, but for apple cakes and pies, you may want the slices to retain some shape.

So, use your own tastebuds to decide whether you will make good use of a variety, not the regurgitations of long lines of books. Remember also that sweetness is as much a result of climate, location and weather as variety and will vary from year to year. Obviously if you hate cooking and baking, you will not want

A froth of cooking apples.

a Bramley or other really sour apple tree, but don't write off every variety described as 'culinary' without questioning, or, better, tasting. It could be just the one you're looking for.

If you are seeking specific fruit to make cider or perry (not pear-flavoured cider), you will probably need to consider more carefully. We have made some superb cider using an eclectic mix of local apples brought to a juicing day. We have also made some undrinkable or insipid cider! Cider from your orchard really will be better if there is a mixture of sharp, bittersweet, sour and sweet apples. If you don't want to grow specific cider varieties, use a mix of apple flavours and favour the ones that yield lots of juice, not dry ones. The Keswick Codlin, Katy and Lord Derby apples are good examples. A good perry flavour is harder to achieve using normal orchard pears, so you might need to specialise in perry pears for that.

Tam Jeffrey, a pretty Scottish apple more suited to cider than desserts.

## Shape and size

Think about what size you want your trees to become when choosing them. How many trees you can fit into a given space will depend on how big they grow, or how you plan to train them. The former usually depends on the rootstock on to which they are grafted, while the latter is up to you – though trained trees need the right rootstock to do well, too. There is a lot more detail about rootstocks in the next chapter, but here is a summary for now.

Apples are available on rootstocks that will allow your choice of tree go to 6m (20ft) tall and spreading,

or to remain a compact 2m (6.6ft) height. They may not all be available in the garden centre, though, which is why a specialist fruit-tree grower is best consulted. Remember, too, that apple varieties vary in vigour, regardless of rootstock. A Bramley on a dwarf rootstock such as M27 will probably be bigger than a Stirling Castle on a semi-vigorous MM106. 'All on the same rootstock' does not mean 'all the same size' in ten years! And the rootstocks vary according to location to some extent. MM106, often referred to as semi-dwarfing, is regarded as semi-vigorous in Scotland, as it results in a larger tree there.

Pears were once described in Scotland as 'pears fir yer heirs', because, when grown on vigorous wild pear rootstock, they can tower up like small oak trees, taking their time to produce bountiful crops of fruit. But grafted on to quince rootstocks, they make a sensible garden-sized tree that can be grown against a south-facing wall, benefiting from the reflected warmth of bricks and rendering without pulling the wall down. Resist buying any fruit tree that does not specify both variety *and* rootstock on the label, however cheap. Even if they do have this information, the labels may prove to be wrong. Mutinous, gangly, non-fruiting plums vaguely labelled 'dwarf Victoria', for example, are very likely to turn out to be plum rootstocks.

For cherries, look for Gisela rootstock if you are short of space, or plan to wall-train them. Colt and Brompton stock are better suited to free-standing

Stirling Castle apple is best on a vigorous rootstock.

trees. If you want plums, gages and damsons, it is worth remembering that these vigorous trees always make quite large specimens on most rootstocks. Pixy is the most dwarf of the available choices.

Usually, trying to wall-train a fruit tree on a vigorous rootstock is a case of storing up trouble and will lead to a lot of work. Choose dwarfing rootstocks for espaliers, fans, stepovers or cordons. Incorporating these restricted forms into your orchard will allow you to get more varieties into the space available, as they do not need such wide spacing, especially cordons. Be aware, though, that dwarfing rootstocks mean less extensive root systems. If your site is windy or exposed, you will be well advised to go for something more vigorous to enable the trees to establish, stay rooted firmly and focused on fruit production.

## Pollination

Fruit trees are usually more productive when cross-pollinated, even those described as self-fertile. Some actually *have* to be cross-pollinated, because they are self-*in*fertile – they cannot accept their own pollen to make fruit. Therefore, when choosing a range of trees, make sure that there are specimens, particularly of apples, the plum family and pears, that will be in flower at the same time, or at least part of the time. In most situations, do not worry, as there will be plenty of neighbouring trees around well within the flight radius of the average bee and the vast majority of varieties flower at least partly in the 'mid' season. You are unlikely to buy a tree that flowers after all of its potential polliniser tree blossoms are finished. More detail will be found in Chapter 6, but for now, be aware that:

- cross-pollination always favours fruit production
- the exact time of flowering varies from year to year and from place to place
- the order in which varieties come into blossom does not change
- some fruit trees (for example, Jargonelle pear and Bramley apple) are triploid – have three sets of chromosomes – and thus need at least two other polliniser partners, not one

Now you have all the information to make good fruit-tree choices and have delved into the variety lists – which may be dictated by what your local supplier has available, of course – or you may be tempted to go one stage further to get exactly the tree you want, by building your own!

Jargonelle pears, when ripe, are very juicy.

## Along the Silk Road

The ancestor of our domestic apple is a species called *Malus sieversii*, which is found in the Tian Shan mountains of Kazakhstan. Here in its native habitat, *M. sieversii* produces a highly diverse array of apples: sweet, sour, large, small, crisp, soft, red, yellow, green. The species carries enormous genetic diversity, which should not surprise us, given the potential for variation in our cultivated varieties.

From this starting point, animals such as bears and wild horses spread the seeds along their migration and foraging routes. These tracks were followed by humans and became the trade routes between China and Europe, passing through the steppes of central Asia. The 'Horse Road' only became known as the Silk Road when the trade in silk became its commonest currency. And as the traders hurried along, they would pick the biggest, juiciest, sweetest apples, then throw away the cores, until the sweet apples established themselves in the Middle East and began to be cultivated there in gardens. On his conquest of Persia in the fourth century BCE, Alexander (the Great) was sufficiently taken with apples to import the fruit and its gardeners into Greece. Apples then travelled from Greece to Rome, where the art of grafting was developed and soon applied to apples.

The rest may be history, but it's not that simple and the Greeks and Romans should not get all the credit. Trade between the Middle East and Celtic Britain existed before the Romans arrived, while grafting was a skill mentioned in the Old Testament and known also in ancient China. It seems unlikely that Celtic apple mythology arose around unpalatable crabs, so it's fair to surmise that some of those Silk Road apples were either selected or grafted in these islands 2,000 years ago or more!

## Chapter Three

# Grafting

In Britain, we almost lost the knowledge and expertise that are needed for fruit production – a body of skills that starts with the propagation of new trees. For very good reasons, this involves the art and craft of grafting. Whilst few people have these skills, we have always found great enthusiasm for our grafting workshops and courses – and there are always participants who, had they not been lawyers/civil servants/accountants and so on, take to it readily and could have had great careers in horticulture! It isn't that difficult in theory, but it does take constant observation, consideration and reflection, trial and error, and a dogged determination to get good at it.

What follows are the methods that work for us. There are other techniques and other propagators will have developed their own. If you want to delve deeper, we would recommend *The Manual of Plant Grafting* by Peter MacDonald,[2] or the classic *The Grafter's Handbook* by R.J. Garner.[3]

## What is grafting?

Grafting is the joining together of two different trees – the rootstock being one and an especially productive scion, or twig, forming the upper part of the tree. The scion is cut from the apple, pear, plum, cherry or other variety that bears the fruit you want to grow – for example, Bramley apple, Victoria plum, Jargonelle pear. The rootstock – which is grown and selected specially for the purpose of being a rootstock – confers attributes of size (dwarfing, semi-dwarfing, vigorous) and early productivity on the newly grafted tree.

You might ask whether you could grow a tree from, say, an apple pip or a cutting. While you could indeed plant an apple pip from your favourite supermarket apple, it's very unlikely to produce fruit that tastes or looks like the original apple. This is because fruit trees are cross-pollinated and the pips from an apple contain the genes from other varieties, or from crab apples. More often than not, if there is fruit at all, it borders on the inedible. We once planted a tree not knowing that we had accidentally been given a rootstock, the grafted variety having died. It grew very big very quickly and produced masses of rock-hard, foul-tasting, mud-coloured apples that not even the mistle thrush wanted to eat. Even pickling scarcely improved them. More on that later!

But it's fair to say that you could get lucky, too. Bramley's Seedling (synonymous in many people's eyes to 'cooking apple') arose in Mr Bramley's garden from just such an experiment – and has been propagated by grafting ever since. There's a wildling tree we know of in a local hedgerow by a walking track that must have arisen from a discarded apple core, which produces rather nice, refreshing green apples every year. And there is an argument for continued experimentation and encouragement of open-pollination in orchards, which might allow the generation of new fruit varieties to have more resilience to climate change or disease, for example.

As for taking cuttings, in theory a fruit tree could be grown on its own roots, if the twigs could be persuaded to produce them. There are some varieties, such as the Oslin (also known as the Arbroath Pippin, an ancient variety brought to eastern Scotland by the monks), which produce aerial roots on the trunk or branches and these take hold readily when put into the ground. Our most enormous cooking apples come from an unnamed tree we were given as a cutting. The disadvantage is that a tree grown 'on its own roots' can also become enormous and you could wait many years before getting a decent crop.

Grafting, therefore, is a skill worth having, and not just for the fun of creating your own tree and getting reliable results. It makes it possible, for example, to 'move' a much-loved mature tree by taking scions to graft on to rootstocks in a new home. It is useful as a way of saving or perpetuating a particularly rare or valuable heritage tree that is threatened. And if you plant a tree and decide the fruit is not worth the space the tree occupies, you can graft better varieties on to it, steadily replacing the original.

## More about rootstocks

Years of research have resulted in the development of rootstocks for all the commoner orchard trees, giving rise to specimens to suit every space or desired form. The rootstocks are designated by names or numbers, which should feature on the labels of all shop-bought fruit trees. If they don't, don't buy!

The main functions of the rootstock are to reduce the size, determine the rate of growth and minimise

Own-root trees are able to grow aerial roots and to become rootstocks.

the time for the tree to reach full production. Rootstocks can be classified as very dwarfing, dwarfing, semi-dwarfing/semi-vigorous, or vigorous. Very dwarfing and dwarfing rootstocks, such as M9 for apples, are suited to commercial production, being very quick to bear fruit, productive and easy to harvest. However, the smaller the root system, the greater the need for staking for the life of the tree. and more care is required with weeding, watering and feeding.

More vigorous rootstocks, such as M111 or M25 in apples and Pear Seedling in pears, will give rise

Rootstocks lined out ready for grafting.

## Table 2: Rootstocks in current use for orchard trees in Britain

| | | |
|---|---|---|
| **Apples** | M27 | Very dwarfing; suitable for producing a tree to grow in a container |
| | M9 | Dwarfing rootstock, suitable for producing a tall, narrow tree |
| | M26 | Good rootstock for an average garden-sized tree |
| | M116 | Suitable for small gardens |
| | MM106 | Semi-dwarfing or semi-vigorous, depending on the variety; produces larger trees, whose fruit may not be reachable from the ground |
| | M111 | Produces a larger tree for a traditional orchard |
| | M25 | Vigorous rootstock; makes a large tree with fruit unreachable from the ground |
| **Pears** | Quince C | Very dwarfing; suitable for closely spaced cordons |
| | Quince A | Dwarfing – suitable for average-sized gardens or espaliers |
| | Pyrodwarf | Despite the name, this rootstock produces a fairly large tree |
| | Pear Seedling/ Kirchensaller | Vigorous rootstock eventually making massive trees for traditional orchards |
| **Plums** | Pixy | Dwarfing rootstock for gardens/fan-trained plums |
| | VVA | Semi-dwarfing; can be used for fans |
| | Wavit | Semi-vigorous rootstock |
| | St Julien | Semi vigorous; can make a large tree |
| **Cherries** | Gisela | Dwarfing rootstock, suitable for cherry trees to be grown under cover |
| | Colt | Semi-vigorous; produces a larger tree |
| | Brompton | Vigorous rootstock |

to a large, spreading tree needing 4–8m (13–26ft) of space, with a deeper and more spreading root system. Long leading shoots and side branches will be produced for a good number of years and fruit production will take longer to start. They can be good rootstocks to use on windy or exposed sites, if regularly pruned, and in large gardens where space and shade are not an issue.

Rootstocks can be purchased online from a few nurseries in winter when they are dormant. They will arrive bare-root and it is preferable to graft them right away, then pot them up afterwards. If that's not possible, or they are already potted up, you will need to manoeuvre around them. Alternatively, plant them out 30–45cm (12–18in) apart, ready for chip budding in the summer (*see* below).

## Before you start …

A bit of plant science. If you're going to graft successfully, you need to understand the importance of the cambium. Whatever the width of the scion – and however massive the trunk of a tree – there is only one part that is actually alive in the sense of being capable of lateral growth. That part is the cambium (*see* diagram), a thin, green layer just under the bark and surrounding the heartwood. As the cambium

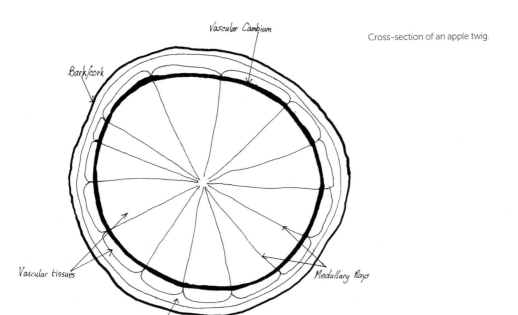

grows outward, the tree or branch increases in girth. When two cut surfaces of compatible twigs are held together, provided that the cambium on one has good contact with the cambium on the other, a 'gluing', or grafting, of the two can result. If one twig is the rootstock and the other a scion, this will create a new tree.

## What is a 'compatible' twig?

To be compatible, firstly, the two twigs need normally to be the same species, or at the least the same genus, that is, pear on pear, apple on apple. You cannot successfully grow pears and apples on the same tree! There are exceptions, like Adam's Broom, which is a grafted hybrid between a purple broom and a laburnum, and in the Middle Ages some monks successfully grafted their pear scions on to hawthorn when they reached Britain (*see* below). But in both these cases, the two 'twigs' were at least in the same botanical family. A sizeable amount of shared genetic material is essential.

Second, the rootstock and scion should be compatible in terms of growth rate. You often see ornamental trees in old gardens that were grafted decades ago,

but look top-heavy, the grafted scions having grown faster than the rootstock. Eventually the rootstock will break under the weight of the tree perching on top of it.

Third, the cuts made in the rootstock and scion in preparation for grafting must match – specifically, the cambium must be in contact, with no gaps that could lead to a weak or deformed graft union.

Successful grafting, in summary, depends on:

- compatibility of rootstock and scion
- choice of disease-free plant material
- correct timing of operation
- speed of insertion/uniting of twigs
- accuracy of cuts
- prevention of movement at the join
- ensuring that the graft union does not dry out

## Choosing good scion material

Scion material (known as 'budwood' when used for bud-grafting) is the collection of twigs taken from the tree, which you want to graft on to rootstock or on to another tree. Your scion material should be:

A poor graft union has developed on this tree.

Well-grafted apple trees.

- **Healthy**  Avoid any growth that shows signs of disease, such as virus or canker, but also aim to take it from a healthy tree. If you're grafting scions from an old or failing tree, this might be tricky. If you can plan fourteen months ahead, give the old tree a hard prune the winter before you graft – this should stimulate the growth of healthy new shoots ideal for scionwood.
- **The current year's growth**  This will be the healthiest and most likely to 'take', or succeed. On fruit trees, new growth will be growing vertically upward and there will be a ring around the twig marking the point where the season of growth began. If you use two-year-old growth, you may get a flowering scion and no growth.
- **Pencil-thick**  The thickness of the scion should roughly match the rootstock or branch on to which you are grafting. It is wise to take the whole current-year shoot – not all of it will be used, but that will give you wiggle-room for getting the perfect size. If you are chip-budding (more later), it will give you the maximum number of buds, too.
- **Fresh**  Use your scion wood as soon as possible after cutting and don't leave it lying around where it can dry out. Grafting straight after pruning is handy – you need to prune out those twigs anyway. If there is any delay at all, wrap the scion wood in a bag and keep it in a fridge or cool place for up to a few weeks. We have had fresh material come through the post well wrapped and stored and have been able to use it successfully. This was not the case when a pile of twigs was left unwrapped on the sunny doorstep by a well-meaning person!

Graftwood ready for use.

sort you tie yourself. A rubberised band can also be used, with a coating of wax to seal. If you are only doing a few trees, you may want to avoid the plastic waste and use traditional raffia and wax to tie up the graft.

- **Water-repellent wax**  This is used for sealing some kinds of graft unions, or with raffia until the graft has taken. It's also used to seal the cut ends of the scion.
- **Sheltered site**  A sheltered site or temporary windbreaks need to be sought out during the grafting period

## Timing and the best types of grafting

Late summer and late winter are the best times for grafting fruit trees. In winter, you will have the advantage of selecting dormant shoots for scions and less risk of them drying out, but you might want to find a

You will also need a variety of tools for grafting:

- **Grafting knife or retractable-blade knife**  A grafting knife is often recommended, but our grafting improved immensely when we changed to a sturdy retractable-blade knife. These have the advantage of an ever-sharp blade and tick the safety boxes. Craft knives are usually too flimsy.
- **Polythene tape**  This is quick and easy to use if you are doing lots of trees, and there are special self-adhering tapes for budding and grafting, although we have had more success with the

Tools for grafting.

weatherproof shed or shelter and work on bare-root rootstocks, potting them up carefully afterwards, rather than work outside. Whip, or whip and tongue, grafting is the most suitable method. If you are grafting on to an existing tree, obviously you can't take it into the shed! Cleft grafting is most suitable for this operation.

In summer, you can do chip budding, which is how new fruit trees are produced professionally. It has a high rate of success and, with practice, can be done quickly and efficiently on a large number of rootstocks. It is usually carried out in the field and your budwood will need to be prepared by removing all foliage when collecting.

### Whip grafting

To carry out whip grafting:

- Choose a scion that is exactly the same diameter as your rootstock.
- Cut the scion to around 5cm (2in), ensuring that there are two to three healthy buds visible on it.
- Using your knife, make a slanting cut at the top of the rootstock, pulling the knife upward in one action and keeping your thumb out of the way! On bare-root rootstocks, you can hold the tree in one hand and cut horizontally. On planted stocks, you must cut upward.
- Make a matching diagonal cut of the bottom of the scion in the same way. Make sure that the buds are pointing upward – it doesn't work if the scion is upside-down!
- The two cuts should be flat and fit perfectly together without gaping holes.
- Fit the scion to the rootstock and tie around fairly tightly with grafting tape.
- Tie both rootstock and scion ends of the new tree to a cane to prevent any movement that will break the union when it forms.

If the rootstock and scion are not a perfect match for size, all is not lost: a side veneer graft uses one side of the rootstock.

## Tip

Getting a perfect match with your cuts is unusual at first – beginner's luck – but becomes easier with practice. Trainees who keep playing with their grafts to improve the fit usually end up making them worse and have to start again. It's best therefore to start at the top of the rootstock so that you have room to do another cut if you make a mistake.

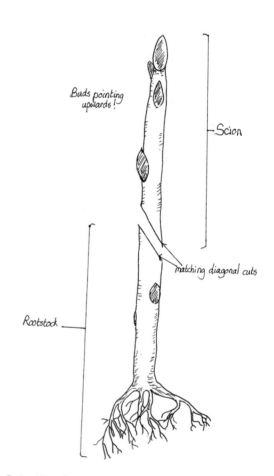

Buds pointing upwards!

Scion

matching diagonal cuts

Rootstock

Basic whip graft.

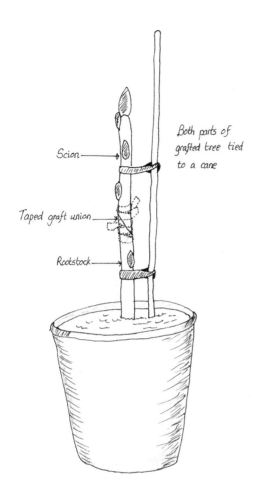

Scion

Both parts of grafted tree tied to a cane

Taped graft union

Rootstock

Completed whip graft.

Use a side veneer graft if your twigs are not of equal thickness.

If you feel confident, you can create a more secure graft union by adapting this method to make a whip and tongue graft. Slice into the middle of each cut to make a sort of woodworking 'biscuit' joint and gently push these together firmly. Wrap the tape tightly to hold the joint in place. Potentially, you will get a new tree in one year by using this method.

Use the cane to tie in the new shoot when it grows. Often two shoots will take off over the summer; if you're confident that one is growing well, it's wise to take one off. Remember, keep your small trees in a sheltered place to prevent wind breakage. Ban playful dogs and children with footballs and too much energy from the area!

## Budding, chip-budding or bud-grafting

In essence, budding is a two-year operation. It is the first choice of most commercial producers who are growing hundreds or thousands of fruit trees every year, but it could also be a good choice if you want to produce your own trees and are aiming for a fair-sized orchard.

Plan for year one:

- **November to January**  Purchase rootstocks. Get the right rootstocks for the size of tree you want. They will arrive bare root; take care not to

Begin the Whip-and-Tongue graft with the whip graft cuts

Scion ←

Rootstock ←

Whip and tongue joint.

Whip and tongue graft with polythene ready to remove.

let the roots dry out if you can't plant right away, by heeling them into soil, bark or compost.

- Plant rootstocks into weed-free soil, or into pots. Use a cane or post to tie in each rootstock.
- **February to August** Feed as required and keep rootstocks weeded and watered.
- **July to August** Collect your budwood – make sure it's healthy – and use the chip-budding method to graft one bud (usually) on to each rootstock. Wrap securely using polythene tape.

Plan for year two:

- **February** Remove the polythene from the graft. (The bud should have 'taken' and not fall off when you do this.)
- Cut back the rootstock in February to just above your bud. This takes skill and practice to get right. 'Feel' for the bud if you cannot see it.
- **April/May onwards** As the grafted bud forms a shoot and grows, remove any buds opening on the rootstock below the graft union – they will *not* be your chosen scion. Carefully tie in the new shoot to a cane or post.
- **December to March** Lift and replant each tree in its permanent position.

## Our bud-grafting technique

Once you've mastered it, budding is a very easy way to produce new trees. The main drawback is waiting until spring to know whether you have been successful. The key to success is speed and accuracy. Choose a good day for budding – you need to work quite quickly to ensure that the buds don't dry out. A blistering hot August day is not ideal, but then neither is a day of drenching summer rain. If you're working on trees planted in the ground, you'll be crouching or bending low – watch that your back is strong enough!

A chip-budded stock.

Budded stock growing away in spring.

This is the procedure that we follow:

- Cut a healthy shoot approximately 25cm (10in) long, of new growth that has started to stiffen, from your chosen tree.
- Trim off all the leaves almost to the stem. The buds lie just above the leaf stalk – be careful not to cut them off.
- If collecting from several trees to use later, keep shoots of each variety in labelled bags in the fridge, until you're ready to start.
- Make a shallow, angled incision into the rootstock, then cut a neat, flat slice downward on the stem about 5cm (2in) from the ground.
- Make a second cut, meeting the first to form a flap at the bottom.
- Take your budwood. Slice with the knife just under a bud towards you and out again, removing the bud with a thin flap of wood behind it.

You are aiming for a bud that fits snugly and is a similar width and length to the cut on the stock, or slightly narrower. If it is not possible to get the cambium to match on both sides, push the bud to one side of the cut – then at least two lines of cambium will be in contact.

Remember:

- Try not to touch the back of the bud – it must be clean and fresh.
- Place the bud into the flap of the rootstock and wrap it up immediately using polythene tape.
- Have polythene cut to 15cm (6in) lengths in advance. Stretch the tape slightly to begin, with a simple crossing-over fold for the tape to grip on itself and be held in place, then start wrapping from the bottom, tightly.
- Take care not to slide the bud from its pocket, dislodge or damage it.
- Twist tape up the stem, covering the bud.
- At the top, secure the tape by coming back down the stem with the last turn and feeding tape through the loop you have made to form a knot.

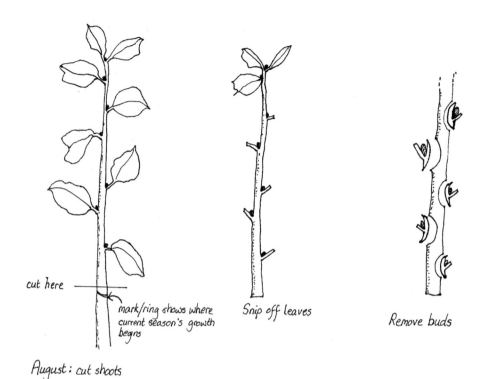

cut here ——— 

mark/ring shows where current season's growth begins

August: cut shoots

Snip off leaves

Remove buds

March: remove polythene

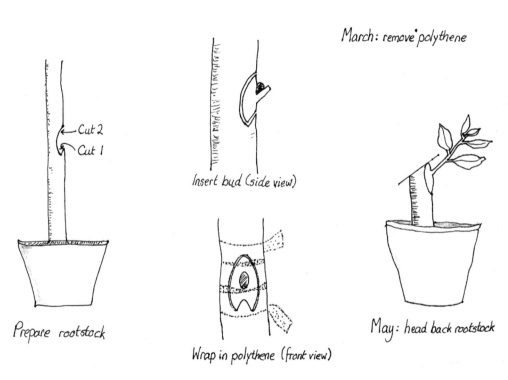

Cut 2

Cut 1

Prepare rootstock

Insert bud (side view)

Wrap in polythene (front view)

May: head back rootstock

Stages in bud grafting.

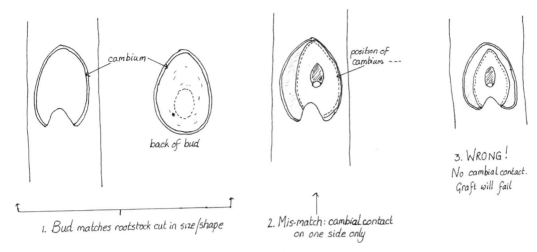

cambium

back of bud

1. Bud matches rootstock cut in size/shape

position of cambium ---

2. Mis-match: cambial contact on one side only

3. WRONG! No cambial contact. Graft will fail

Ensure cambial contact between bud and rootstock.

## Tip

Stretch and twist the tape at the end to tighten the whole thing.

Budding nearly complete.

If your buds fail, it is usually because the bud has dried out. This is usually because of poor execution of cuts, or because the bud was not inserted quickly enough into the stock. Not tying tightly enough is another problem. Even when a bud has taken, you must still be careful – it can easily be knocked off as it starts to grow while you're furiously weeding your lovely new tree. And if you don't remember to rub out any competing shoots from the rootstock, they will overwhelm the graft. So be watchful!

## Top-working and cleft grafting

This is the technique to use if you want to change the variety of an older tree, or create a family tree – essentially two or more varieties grafted on to one rootstock. Remember that rootstock we mentioned above, growing nasty, muddy bullets instead of apples in our garden? We had two choices, dig it out (which

Cleft grafting is a good way to create a family tree.

would require a lot of effort, given the size it had grown to and the likely depth of the M25 roots), or transform it. To that end, Andrew grafted twenty-seven varieties on to its branches over the years, most of which took. A few may have been lost in pruning (such as the Lord Derby which was so vigorous it blocked the doorway to the summerhouse and Margaret reluctantly pruned it off). Andrew is still working away at this project and the technique he uses is cleft grafting. Here's how:

- Work in winter, when the trees are dormant. February is ideal.
- Select pencil-thick twigs carrying a couple of good buds of your scion variety, cut to 5cm (2in) or so. Keep in the fridge until you are ready.
- In late February, cut off the end of a branch on your rootstock tree.

- Into the cut end, cut a slit or cleft around 5cm (2in) deep (a hacksaw may be used if it's a stout branch).
- Make two slices about 3cm (1.2in) long on the scion, forming a two-sided point.
- Prise open the cleft and push in the first scion, leaving a small 'window' showing the sliced ends.
- Repeat on the other side of the cleft, using another scion, if there's room. Tipping the scions outward away from each other very slightly helps to ensure contact between the lines of cambium. You should be able to see the exposed green cambium on both stock and scion.
- Wrap the branch in polythene strips where the cut surfaces are and smear with grafting wax (or other water-repellent substance), while not allowing it to get into the cleft and between the scion and the rootstock branch.

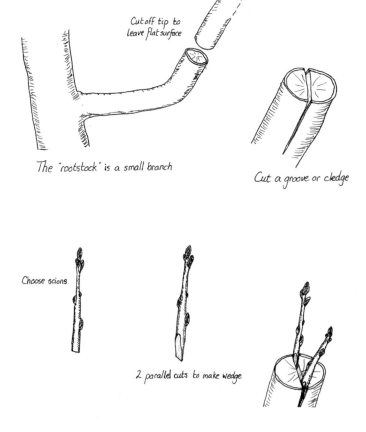

Cut off tip to leave flat surface

The "rootstock" is a small branch

Cut a groove or cledge

Choose scions

2 parallel cuts to make wedge

Cleft grafting.

It is possible for the graft to become dislodged by the wind, or the antics of overweight wood pigeons, but, all being well, you should see some buds opening in spring. If that's followed by extension growth of the scion and both parts growing thicker together, the graft has taken and you could expect flowers and fruit from your grafted variety the following year.

All in all, grafting is fun and fascinating and a skill well worth having for anyone with an orchard.

As you gain confidence, you will enjoy experimenting and refining your technique. Working with knives carries risks, of course, so follow the advice in the diagrams on where your thumb should be. Always use sharp blades of good quality and watch where they're lying when not in use. Work quickly, but don't get flustered – this can make you careless. And enjoy yourself!

## Wandering monks carrying twigs

The spread of Christianity across Europe and the rising ambition of the monastic orders contributed hugely to the establishment in Britain of some of our oldest and most iconic varieties of pear – and apple, too. Cistercian, Benedictine, Tironensian and other orders of monks established in continental Europe sought to expand their influence – and riches – by setting up 'sister houses' in Scotland, England, Wales and Ireland. The monks were a resourceful breed, as was necessary in medieval times, and grew most of their own food. Every abbey had its farms, gardens and orchards and the monks were learned in the skills of grafting.

When a deputation set off to establish a new house in Britain, the monks would bring them the makings of new orchards, in the form of scions from their best trees for grafting. Journeys were long, so graftwood was usually moved in winter, when the sticks, carefully wrapped in damp moss, were dormant. Once arrived, they would need to be grafted quite quickly, but Britain in the Middle Ages lacked handy horticulturists supplying wild pear or quince rootstock. The monks must have deduced that a successful graft relies on the rootstock being as closely related as possible to the scion, so they chose hawthorn, as pears, apples and hawthorn are at least all in the rose family. We find it remarkable that they succeeded, given the challenges of grafting pears on to anything bar wild pear!

So arose around abbey lands a range of local pears, often with French or Belgian-sounding names initially, though these soon became localised. Warden pears, intended for cooking only, were among the earliest, with Catillac and Black Worcester among their descendants. The famous Jedburgh pears, which began with the abbey there, include White Warden. Longueville (Longavil in Scotland) is purported to have arrived with the Black Douglas from his lands in Longueville, France. The hardy Hessle, or Hazel Pear of northern England, gave its name to villages in the fruitful Clyde Valley. Among the many prolific, tall old pear trees of the Carse of Gowrie, which developed in this Tironensian offshoot of Kelso Abbey lands, are some redoubtable Scottish pears, such as Grey Benvie, Craig's Favourite, The Flower of Monorgan, Fair Maid and the beautiful Goudknap (or Gold Knob, which is what it looks like).

Goudknap pears.

## Chapter Four

# A Time to Plant

If a tree is planted well, it has at least an even chance of growing well, even in the most exposed locations, but a tree that is planted roughly, sloppily, or in too much haste is very likely to suffer setbacks in growth and productivity. When asked to advise on a tree or orchard that's not performing as expected, the first thing we look at is the base of the tree. So often the tell-tale evidence of planting damage and problems with root establishment can be seen right away.

## Think before planting

Planting your orchard should not start with a spade and a bag of trees, but with a little thinking! These are some of the things to consider before you start to plant:

- Is the orchard going to need a shelter belt of trees to protect it from howling gales? If so, get the shelter belt planted first.
- Some fruit trees will always be taller, regardless of rootstock. Plums, however meticulously you prune them, will every year put on a lot of tall, straggly growth, often quite dense. Pears on vigorous rootstocks can tower over more dwarfed apples and most plums. Taller trees will shade smaller trees, so look where the light is coming from and don't block off the sun from your dwarf apples or sun-hungry cherries by inserting a giant plum tree. Basically, keep smaller-growing trees roughly to the sunny south side of taller ones.

- Some fruit trees will cope better with exposure to wind and cold than others. These include cherry-plums and damsons. If part of your site is unprotected by windbreaks or buildings, these are the trees to put in there.
- If any part of the site is in more shade than the rest, once again, damsons, plums and gages will be better choices here than apples and pears, which need long seasons of sunlight to ripen well.
- Save the sunniest spots for rosy, bright red eating apples and luscious pears, where they will maximise flavour and juiciness.
- Pears, on vigorous Pear Seedling rootstocks, have a rather surprising tolerance of waterlogged soils, which may be a fact worth knowing in some situations.

If you are planting a fair number of trees, it really is worth drawing up a sketch plan first to decide what goes where. Note down the relative amounts of shade, sun, soil moisture, exposure and so on, then superimpose the names of the trees you will put there.

### Spacing

The space between each tree will be dictated mostly by the rootstock (*see* Chapter 3) and how you plan to train the trees (*see* Chapter 2 and, for more detail, Chapter 5). Unless you are going for very dwarf trees or restricted forms, a reasonable aim is 3m (10ft) between each free-standing tree. Also, be sure to allow for the width of your mower between trees.

If you are planting in straight rows, laying out string lines of course will be a great help. If the trees are to be planted by a community group, it really is worthwhile having the positions of the trees marked out with posts before everyone descends enthusiastically to plant trees. Otherwise, be ready to herd cats when it comes to getting volunteers to space the trees correctly!

## Tip

Rather than getting tangled in surveyors' tape measures or rulers, we like to work in 'spade lengths' (times one, two, or three) from tree to tree. After all, the spade has to go with you when planting, so why carry extra gear?

## When to plant

Ideally, all broadleaved trees should be planted when they are dormant and not growing. That means in winter, from December through to the middle of March. That is not the same as spring, which is a shame because spring is the time when people get a notion to plant orchards. Planting in winter means far less stress to the tree, a greater chance of establishment and survival when done properly and you can purchase your trees as bare-root specimens, which are cheaper, easier to handle and quicker to plant.

When setting a planting date, remember that warm spells in November or March may mean the trees are in growth and therefore not dormant, while the risk in January is that the ground may be frozen solid. It is much better to plan to be flexible! If, for whatever reason, you are delayed and the trees have started into growth before you plant them, then plant container-grown trees instead and take extra precautions with watering before and after planting.

## Planting – step by step

### Plant the post

Most trees, unless in a really sheltered spot, will be supported by tree stakes or posts for the first few years at least. Choose, for preference, a round post, as these will be less likely to damage the tree if it later rubs against the post in high winds.

The purpose of a tree stake is not primarily to hold the trunk straight, but to hold the root ball securely in the soil. If the root ball rocks about, the roots may fail to establish and the tree will not thrive. Once those roots have taken hold, most trees will not need a stake anymore. However, we would advise that productive trees on very dwarfing rootstocks are staked throughout their whole life. This is not to hold the root ball still, but to tie in the leading shoot, thus helping to train the tree and to hold up branches that are laden with fruit to stop them from breaking.

Angled posts can be used for trees supplied in pots, but these can be difficult to put in and 'fit' to the tree, so we rarely advise their use. Double stakes with a crossbar are suitable for very large trees, but are no real advantage for most fruit trees. For trees on vigorous rootstocks, look for a tall, round post, maximum diameter 100mm (4in). Whatever size of

New orchard trees require good staking.

stake you use, it is important that at least one-third of the total length is in the ground.

Using a good spade, mark a rough circle a bit wider than the size of the tree's spread roots, then lift out the turf into a wheelbarrow. (This turf can be inverted in a pile under a hedge or suitable spot, where it will eventually decompose to form good loam.) If you are on 'claggy' clay soil, avoid smooth edges to the planting hole, which may prevent roots from exploring beyond it. Loosen the edges with a fork and even make the circle nearly square, encouraging roots into the corners and then beyond.

## Tip

A good spade is sharp and has a protective wide tread atop the blade. This saves your boots (and your feet) from being damaged during digging.

Dig out the soil to a spade's depth, putting this aside for refilling. Place this soil on a bag or in a barrow, rather than risk losing it in the long grass. You will often find that there is mysteriously less soil for refilling than you took out; a useful solution to this perplexing dilemma is to mentally locate a few useful molehills to compensate for any shortage if needed.

Provided that there are no obstructions, position the post on the windward side of the tree. This is to avoid high winds blowing the young tree against the post and damaging the bark. Then hammer in the stake or post firmly, taking care to ensure that it is upright and not out of line if planting in rows. One post out of line, or leaning at a weird angle, can be infuriating! If the soil is very hard or stony, make a pilot hole first using a pinch bar. We have seen many split mashed-up tops of tree stakes, especially where poorer quality wooden stakes are used. Use a club hammer, a heavy maul, or a fencing drive-all (a big heavy metal cylinder with two handles – difficult to use if you're not used to it, but

Put the post in first and then the tree.

effective if you have lots of posts to put in). Make sure that the post is really firm – if there's some obstruction and it's not, take it out and put it in a slightly different spot.

Why plant the post first? If you plant the tree first, you are bound to then drive the post through its

Unstaked trees can fall over with the weight of fruit.

roots, causing damage. It can be tricky when planting trees from pots, as the roots could be solidly meshed together and hard to spread apart. Unless there is no other option, you may need to force the post through to get it close enough to tie.

## Is the tree ready to plant?

In frost-free conditions, remove with secateurs any shoots or suckers from below the graft union before planting. A tree that is 'feathered' with branches low down the stem may need a branch or two cut off to sit snugly against the post.

Until you are ready to plant, keep the tree in its pot or in a bag. Wind or sun will dry the tree's roots out very quickly. Take the tree out at the last minute and check that the hole you have dug is deep and wide enough. Spread the roots, uncurling any that have circled around inside a pot. It is safe to trim back any particularly long roots, so long as an even spread of roots in all directions is achieved. The graft union should be just above finished soil level. Use a spade laid across the hole to confirm this will be the case. Most of a fruit tree's roots will be in the top 30cm (12in) of soil, so there will rarely be the need to dig much more than a spade's depth. Once the hole is big enough, it's time to plant.

## Planting the tree

- Rotate the tree in the hole until it sits snugly near the post and is upright. On a windy site, point any long branches into the teeth of the wind. It is difficult to get good growth in this direction, so start the tree with an advantage.
- Start to backfill the hole, shaking the tree a little to begin with to ensure that some of the soil goes underneath the root ball.
- Firm gently with your fingers or the toe of a boot, but be careful not to bruise the main stem

base of the trunk as you go and especially when using a spade to backfill.
- Firm as you go, working quickly to avoid roots drying out, but ensuring that there are no air pockets under the surface – roots will only grow when in contact with soil. Finished soil level should be just below the graft union.

## Attaching the tree tie

Rubber tree ties with buckle and spacer should be used to secure the tree to the post. *Never* use cable ties, wire, baler twine, or any material than cannot be adjusted as the tree grows. Make sure that the rubber spacer is positioned between the post and the tree as shown to create a figure of eight – two circles, one around the stake, one around the tree. The tree *must not* be tied against the stake and touching, as the bark will be rubbed away and the tree will probably die. Better to forget the stake and tie altogether than to do that.

Do not nail the tie to the stake (or, obviously, to the tree!). If you think the tie is in danger of slipping down, you could hammer a nail into the post below the tie. Position the tie as near to the top of the stake as you can, as this will minimise the risk of the tree rubbing against the post in high winds.

Good planting and happy trees at Kirkfieldbank Community Orchard, Clyde Valley.

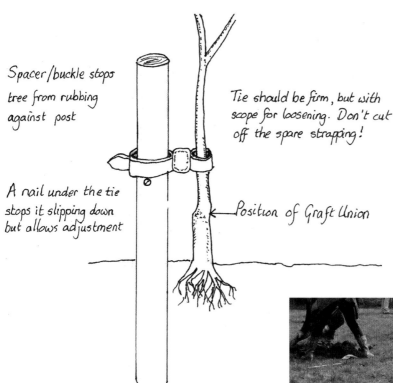

Spacer/buckle stops tree from rubbing against post

Tie should be firm, but with scope for loosening. Don't cut off the spare strapping!

A nail under the tie stops it slipping down but allows adjustment

Position of Graft Union

Stake and tie.

Makeshift tree ties can be created from bicycle inner tubes, flexible rubber hosing and even old tights, so long as you remember the need for a figure of eight design with a space and the need to adjust or remove the ties before they strangle the tree.

## Guard and guard well

There are a number of animals that will damage your tree if they get access to it, but the main ones are rabbits, voles, sheep, deer and humans with strimmers or mowers. These are described further in Chapter 10. The kinds of guard needed will vary according to which of the above presents the greatest risk.

To start with the smallest, vole damage is often overlooked, or not anticipated. You will normally be planting in winter, when voles are not only hungriest, but also happy to hide in tree shelters or under mulch mats nestled up to a food source – the base of your

Dwarf posts can be effective.

Some vole guards are strong enough for strimmer protection, too.

Rabbit guards are generally essential.

cherished apple tree! A solid vole guard 15cm (6in) high inserted *into* the soil around the trunk usually discourages them.

Rabbits are expected and again will be most damaging in winter. A flexible spiral rabbit guard that allows the tree to breathe is a minimum requirement when planting in open areas, whether rural or urban. Be aware that if your area gets heavy snowfall, rabbits are adept at climbing snowdrifts to gnaw at the bark above guard level. Two spiral guards atop each other may work. It may be tricky positioning them around low shoots and branches, so consider cutting these off. DIY rabbit guards formed individually from rolled plastic, or galvanised metal chicken wire cut to size and rolled loosely, then secured with canes or narrow stakes can be made to any height and may be more effective if bunnies are a serious issue.

Deer are monstrously fond of fruit trees. They will eat young shoots within their reach, rub against the bark and even eat it when hungry enough. Install either ready-made or DIY deer guards to protect your trees, but remember that as these need to be 1.8–2m (6–6.6ft) tall, you will be obliged to grow standard trees of a greater height than maybe you planned. In this case, consider seriously deer and rabbit fencing the perimeter of the entire orchard – not forgetting the gate!

Sheep (and other livestock) will not only nibble at the trees, but knock them over by rubbing against them, or, in the case of lambs, using them as play equipment. Horses with itchy backs are terrors for rubbing the bark away from even well-established trees. If you must have livestock in your orchard, we suggest you plant vigorous standard trees and

Rabbit damage can occur above a standard spiral guard.

A taller guard can better protect against rabbits and voles.

build a substantial timber cage around each tree to ensure that the beasts won't get near them. (But remember that the voles still can, so don't leave off the vole guards.) Poultry are all right in well-established orchards, though chickens will scratch away the soil from young tree roots, which challenges the growth of the trees. They will also jump up and peck at low-hanging fruit. Try to avoid the tall forestry-type plastic tree shelters, as they do not allow access for pruning off any lower branches that arise.

Think carefully about the rogue human. Who is going to maintain the sward? Are they competent, careful, likely to listen? Creating a 1m (3.3ft) wide, weed-free mowing circle around each tree may be a good preventive measure if you have a mower-mad grass maintainer. It will also reduce grass and weed competition if combined with grass and weed-suppressing mulching materials, such as mats made of fabric, straw, bark or other options as available. Strimmers should never get anywhere near your trees – the stake only protects on one side – and it is extraordinary how unaware some folk can be of the reach of strimmer cord when the engine's whirring. Conventional forestry tree tubes are not strimmer-proof and, as noted above, are not necessarily the best solution for orchard trees.

Well-designed DIY tree guards can be excellent for everything from voles to deer.

Stronger timber and posts are needed to protect trees against livestock.

Be warned! Sheep love apple wood for dinner.

Rabbit netting and a sturdy vole guard may be the better option.

Use whatever you have to hand to mulch your trees.

## Water, water

If you are planting in winter as you should be, the ground should be moist and watering each newly planted tree may be superfluous – although with climate change, droughts in early spring are not uncommon and a good slosh of water will never do any harm after planting. If you are planting outside the trees' dormant period, watering is absolutely crucial.

You may need to water the ground before as well as after planting – and as the trees will be in pots at this time, make sure that the pots are very well watered before you take them out. During the early months of establishment, continue to water well regularly, especially if a spring drought occurs.

## Feeding, mulching and manuring

Unless the soil you are planting into is really awful, infertile, despoiled or a mass of stones, it is best *not* to mix in manure, nice rich compost or special treats for the trees. Backfilling with the native soil helps the young tree to adapt to local conditions and is likely to result in better root growth and establishment in the long run. The roots of trees planted into choice garden-centre compost act a bit like house-plant roots in a pot – they will go round and round in circles trying to stay in the nice cosy 'pot' rather than access the harsher but better life outside. Fresh manure is the worst, as it can heat up and produce acids that will damage the roots. It can also form a wet, rotting mass, creating anaerobic conditions. Roots need oxygen as well as water and nutrients, so will therefore die back.

The other thing to remember is that if you are planting in winter and the trees are dormant, it won't be until the spring that they will have the fine roots that can take up the nutrients you kindly add to the planting hole in the form of fertiliser. By that time, those nutrients will largely have washed away in the rain. So, it makes more sense to give the trees a top dressing of something organic and slow release such as bonemeal, well-matured garden compost or poultry manure pellets to stimulate root growth *in early spring*, instead of cosseting them pointlessly while they are asleep. However, mulching slow-release organic matter into the mowing circle after planting can be beneficial if the soil is very poor.

## The magic of mycorrhizae

What bonemeal supplies that is so good for stimulating root growth is phosphorus. Given how deficient most soils are in phosphorus, you have to wonder how trees – or any plant come to that – have become so successful and are such an integral part of how this planet works. For centuries, humans have overlooked the extraordinary relationship between trees and the soil-dwelling fungi associated with them. Fungi grow as an underground web of ultra-thin filaments known as hyphae (collectively called the mycelium). Some of the hyphae encase the tips of the roots of trees and some enter into the roots. Far from doing damage, they mostly proceed to supply the plant with phosphorus and allow it to access a far richer seam of essential nutrients than it could on its own, while benefiting from the association by sharing in the sugars and carbon metabolised by the plant. It is unlikely that land plants would ever have evolved without the help of fungi.

Almost all plants, including orchard trees, have one or several fungal mycelia living with them. This conglomeration of roots and mycelium is called mycorrhizae (literally, 'fungus-roots'). Field-grown fruit trees will have already acquired some fungal friends from the minute the rootstocks are planted, without any effort on the grower's part, so long as the soil is healthy and not subject to regular drenching in pesticides. However, when trees are sold bare-root, most of the soil and any mycorrhizal roots will be lost. And when trees are sold in pots of garden compost, the right fungi are very unlikely to be present. Therefore, it makes sense to add mycorrhizae in powdered form when planting your tree. Fruit-tree mycorrhizae even help to protect trees from the effects of replant disease and other problems (*see* Chapter 11). Several companies have discovered that selling dried mycorrhizae is good business for them. Before deciding whether to go down this route, please be aware that:

- The fungi that have beneficial association with fruit trees are fairly specific – it's not a case of 'one size fits all'. Does the proprietary mycorrhizal mix contain the right mushrooms?
- If you are planting into healthy, organic soil that is teeming with life and not with fungicide, insecticide, herbicide and chemical stimulants, the right fungal mycelium will find its way to your trees in due course and build a solid relationship.

Your decision as to whether or not to add mycorrhizae may therefore depend on the condition and treatment of your soil.

## Forbidden fruit

From the sacred apple trees and paradise orchards discussed earlier, somehow the poor old apple got into bad company and became a byword for poison, sin and trouble. Think of Snow White. In this German folk tale, a princess is poisoned by taking a bite from the red side of a bicoloured apple (though in one version it's a pear) and falls into a coma. The fruit is synonymous with deceit, wickedness and attempted murder.

The story began because of a dispute about who was 'the fairest of them all' and this is also the theme behind the most troublesome apple in the tales of ancient Greece. Three Greek goddesses, Hera, Athene and Aphrodite, each claimed to be the most beautiful. The goddess of discord, Eris, took a golden apple from the Garden of the Hesperides and offered it as a prize for the fairest. They quarrelled endlessly, presumably having nothing better to do, and in the end asked a mortal man – a Trojan called Paris – to decide to whom the golden apple should be awarded.

Paris found this a poisoned chalice in itself, as each amoral goddess sought to make sure of victory by bribery. Hera thought Paris might like to become a powerful ruler, while Athene tried to buy his vote with promises of great military victories. But Aphrodite, goddess of love, promised Paris the most beautiful mortal woman on Earth. Unfortunately, this turned out to be the wife of King Menelaus, Helen of Sparta. When Paris absconded with Helen to Troy, he also incurred the enmity of all the Greek warriors. A thousand ships were launched to chase after them and bring Helen back. Hera was so incensed at losing to Aphrodite that she intervened on the side of the Greeks. Thus began the ten-year Trojan War, which led to the sacking of Troy. It cost Paris his life, along with countless others. All for a golden apple! But it did also give rise to some great stories – the *Iliad* and the *Odyssey*.

And then, look what happened to the apple's reputation in the Book of Genesis as translated and then re-storied into English. The sacred apple tree has become the Tree of the Knowledge of Good and Evil. The dragon from the Avalon tales has become a serpent personified as the Devil. Adam and Eve are forbidden by God to eat the apples from this tree. Eve rebels and, encouraged by the serpent, eats an apple. She scrumps one for Adam as well. This leads to The Fall and being cast out of Eden. Adam and Eve are duly punished, or maybe rewarded, with sex, hard work, mortality – and knowledge. 'A bite of the apple' has become a term synonymous with doing something either naughty or very nice. Drinking the fermented juice even more so – think of Laurie Lee's classic autobiography, *Cider with Rosie*. Do note, though, as Genesis was a tale handed down from the Middle East, the forbidden fruit is unlikely to have been an apple. They don't grow there. Apples are innocent, but some other fruit is implicated!

## Chapter Five

# The Early Years

Now that your trees are perfectly planted, the work begins! The next few years are crucial to how successful your orchard will be. If you think you've done all you need now and leave the trees to grow with no intervention, you will most likely end up with round-headed trees consisting of dense thickets of branches. They will be lopsided, heavy at the top and with lots of dead, diseased, shaded branches at the bottom and in the middle. You see many trees like that in gardens, but never in commercial orchards. A well-pruned and trained tree will have open, regularly spaced branches, with lots of sunlight reaching all parts.

## The basics of pruning

To quote Joan Morgan in *The New Book of Apples*,[4] it will 'take three or four years to establish the form of the tree, which is maintained by annual pruning'. Now you are at the start of those early years and the pruning you are to do is known as formative – getting that desired shape. The key to all formative pruning is to control the head of the tree, which may involve operations such as bending and tying down, tying in young branches to canes to straighten them, or rubbing out buds. Pruning, or cutting to remove shoots, is just one tool in the box of formative training.

Pruning – whether formative at the start of the tree's life, annual summer and winter pruning, or restorative pruning for neglected trees – is focused on getting more of the wood on which flowers are borne, and this varies with each variety, so you need to observe where flowering takes place. The flowering

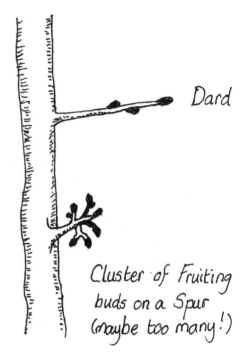

Encourage fruiting wood, dards and spurs.

This tree has flowers on spurs, brindilles and dards along the branch.

shoots – spurs, brindilles and dards – may be borne on wood that is one, two or three years old.

Some varieties, such as the apple Sunset, produce a lot of spurs all along their branches, so you would aim to produce a strong framework of lateral branches starting at 80cm (32in) to 1m (3.3ft) high. These short laterals are pruned back to a stub, in rotation, to form new fruiting spurs. Other varieties, such as Worcester Pearmain apples, flower and fruit on the tips of the branches and are known as 'tip-bearers'. The more tips there are, the more apples. So, the sublaterals in this case must be allowed to become the longer shoots called dards and brindilles, facilitating flower clusters on the ends of each shoot. Every few years, cut back and allow new shoots to appear, in rotation as above. Be aware that pears also can be tip or spur-bearing, so do be observant – where are those flowers appearing? You will find lots more guidance on summer, winter and restorative pruning in Chapters 7 and 9.

## Become aware of the buds

Knowing where to start requires you to imagine where the growth of the tree is going to happen in the next few years. The branches, which are already there, may not be where you need them to be in five years' time. (You can choose whether to leave them to fruit for a few years as temporary branches, or to prune them out straight away.)

So, look at the buds. They will be next year's new branches and you need to identify the ones that will grow into lateral branches heading in the right direction. These will grow your tree to the shape, or 'form', that you want.

It is never too early to calculate the intentions of buds on a new fruit tree. Assess where you will need to prune even before you plant the tree; in fact, even before you buy it! Can that healthy but wildly branching, stocky tree be persuaded into a cordon? Can that 'stick' be made productive?

## What form?

Almost any healthy tree can be trained to any form. The questions are how long can you wait for it to:

- fill its allotted space and
- produce regular large quantities of fruit?

Spur-bearing pear flowering on short shoots along its branches.

If you want quick results, the age of tree you buy and your budget will be a consideration. Older trees cost more, and ready trained trees more still, as several years of skilled nursery work have already been invested in them. If you decide to train a young tree to a desired form yourself, remember to buy trees on the right rootstock. Following are explanations of the most popular forms.

## Restricted space forms

**Espalier:** branches trained horizontally to left and right of the main stem, usually against a wall or fence.

**Cordon:** planted at an angle of 45–60 degrees against a wall or fence.

**Fan:** two or three main stems fanned out from a low point against a wall or fence.

Espaliered pear against a warm wall.

Cordon pears on very dwarfing Quince C rootstocks.

**Stepover:** single- or double-branched tree trained horizontally very low along the ground, often edging a border.

## Open space forms

**Standard:** tree with a round head, with at least three branches radiating from a clear main stem at least 90cm (35in) from the ground.

**Low standard or bush:** as standard, but with branches emerging from a clear stem about 50cm (20in) from the ground. Beware: a 'bush' is also what you get if you leave a plum, apple, pear or quince to 'do its own thing' and grow naturally. A mop-headed bush is not desirable in terms of tree health or productivity, so try to form it into one of the following:

- **Spindle bush:** tree with a central leader and branches wider at the bottom, making an A-shape profile. A tree from the nursery that already has lower branches is described as 'feathered'.
- **Pyramid:** also A-shape in profile, a term often used to describe a more dwarf tree.

Stepovers are a useful way to mark path edges.

Standard trees are ideal for community spaces where mowing is carried out.

- **Open centre or goblet:** round-headed tree with the leader and central branches removed.
- **Straight-lead:** nursery term for a two year-old tree with a tall, straight leader about 2m (6.6ft) high, usually grown on to form a standard or tall spindle bush.

## How to train trees to restricted forms

There are a couple of principles to bear in mind. First, it is perhaps not surprising how few of us realise that trees and branches grow in length *only* from their tips

A fan and two stepovers.

Low standard apple trees are just about okay for mowing around.

Nice triangular-shaped spindle-bush tree.

Open-centred trees in a commercial orchard.

and expand in girth *only* from the cambium under the bark. Therefore, a branch shooting out from the trunk at 30cm (12in) height will *always* be at 30cm. It will not travel further up the trunk because the trunk is not growing from there, only from the tip. Keeping this in mind will help you to imagine where the next and following years' growth will be. Second, you need to be able to recognise one-, two- and three-year-old wood or shoots. At the end of a year's growth, a ring can be seen on every twig, marking the point where growth began and finished that year. This will help you to choose where to prune.

Being able to train a fruit tree against a wall or fence can be a great advantage in terms of space economy, in addition to the benefits gained from the extra warmth, especially from a south-facing wall. Cordons, espaliers and fans are all ideal for this and are great fun to achieve and maintain. Make sure that you do not select a tip-bearer (a tree that bears fruit mostly on the tips of its branches) for training, as you will be removing most of the tips. Apples Discovery and Worcester Pearmain and pear Jargonelle are examples of tip-bearers, but your nursery supplier should be able to tell you about the trees you are buying.

Choosing a maiden tree (a one-year-old unbranched tree) gives you many options regarding which buds to encourage to grow laterally; if you start with a feathered or branching tree, some initial winter pruning to remove the branches going in the wrong directions will be needed. Thereafter, only summer tipping is required routinely. Note that to train your restricted trees, you will need wires, posts, pegs and tensioners.

## Cordons

Cordons are possibly the easiest restricted form to achieve. You must start with trees on dwarfing rootstocks, for example M9 or M26 for apples, or Quince C for pears. Plant preferably as maidens at an angle between 45 and 60 degrees initially, at spacings as close as 1m (3.3ft), or even less. If your chosen tree is too tall, it may have no buds on the lower stem. In this case, you will need to cut it back to 1m (3.3ft), or lower.

Tie the young tree to a long garden cane or similar, otherwise it will immediately try to straighten itself up. Use soft, flexible materials to tie-in – and remember to remove these temporary ties once the wood has

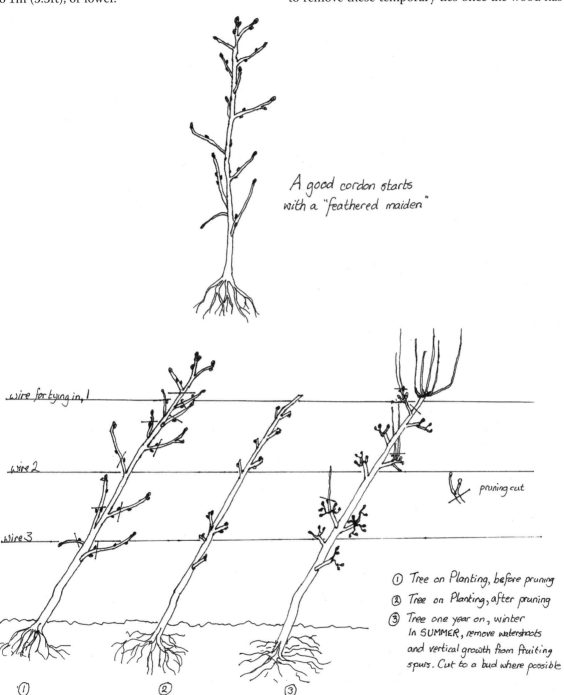

A good cordon starts with a "feathered maiden"

wire for tying in, 1

wire 2

wire 3

pruning cut

① Tree on Planting, before pruning
② Tree on Planting, after pruning
③ Tree one year on, winter
   In SUMMER, remove watershoots and vertical growth from fruiting spurs. Cut to a bud where possible

①          ②          ③

First stages in training a cordon.

lignified, or hardened, in year two. Allow all buds to grow in the first year, except those growing towards the wall if you are using one. Apples and pears are more suited to wall training than plums and cherries, which are more wayward in their growth habit. Next summer, cut back the new lateral branches – which will be trying to grow vertically – to two or three buds close to the main stem. This is called stubbing and will encourage more laterals with fruiting buds at their tips, on what will become a fruiting spur. Tie in the leader to the cane as it grows and cut the leader shoot in winter as soon as it reaches the top of the wall or fence. Each summer, upright shoots are cut back again and the fruiting spurs get larger and more productive, whilst the tree itself remains small and manageable. Strong, upright shoots in the top must be cut off regularly.

There is a special form of cordon that is grown as an upright, or columnar, tree, which is understandably popular in the garden centres. A miniature tree like this, which fruits in a large container, makes the patio or balcony orchard a possibility! A Minarette® tree is trained much the same way as a traditional cordon, only vertically – but note that the name Minarette is trademarked. (So is the term Ballerina®, but a Ballerina® tree from the garden centre has not been trained; it will be one of a limited number of varieties grown as natural miniature sports.) If you want to train your own columnar trees, stick to apples on M27 rootstocks and possibly a few pear varieties on Quince C – we shudder to think of the pandemonium of tangled branches likely to ensue from trying to do this to a plum or cherry.

## Espaliers

Espaliers look very impressive and will take a bit longer to achieve than cordons, but are created using the same principles. You are aiming for regularly spaced, horizontal branches to the left and right of the main trunk and from top to bottom of a wall or fence. Here is an example scenario of the production

of a perfect espalier, though do remember that every tree is different, so adapt as needed:

- A maiden or one-year-old pear tree is to be trained on a 1.8m (6ft) high wall.
- If it's already fairly tall, trim it back to 1m (3.3ft).
- Three branches have formed 30–35cm (12–14in) up the stem, first one going left, second one right and the third points outward 20cm (8in) from the wall. They are at 45-degree angles from the leading stem.
- The third branch is pruned back to a 1–2cm (0.4–0.8in) stub to form a little fruiting spur in the future.
- The first and second branches are tied to a permanent wire (the lowest) on the wall, using flexible ties that will expand with the tree's growth and not damage it. Possibly, the second branch is stronger, so will be tied almost horizontally to slow down its growth rate. The weaker first branch is encouraged to grow more, so is tied to the wire, but pointing slightly upward. The following winter, these branches can be dropped to a more horizontal angle before the wood lignifies.
- The leading shoot that grew in year one now needs to be cut back to encourage the next tier of branches to form. It is cut *above* a bud, at around 60cm (24in) height from the ground. This strong bud will become the new leader.
- Cutting back the leader encourages new lateral branches to grow from buds about 15cm (6in) below the cut in the next year. The two buds just below the new chosen tip, however, are the most dominant now and could grow vigorously to form a narrow, upright, weak crotch in the tree's structure, so these are picked off with thumb and forefinger. With these removed, others lower down will be encouraged to open up.

In future years, each new tier is formed in the same way from the bottom up and trained on to the wires,

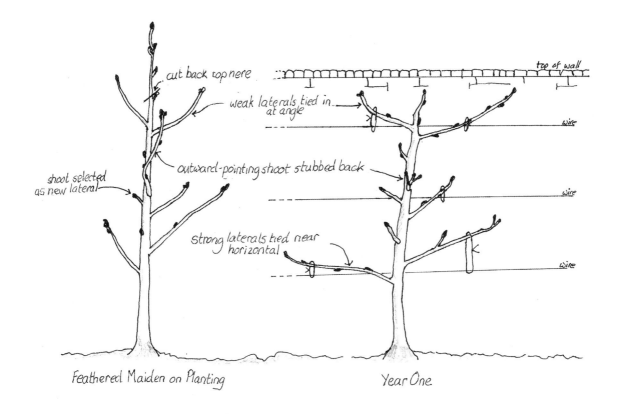

cut back top here

weak laterals tied in at angle

top of wall

wire

shoot selected as new lateral

outward-pointing shoot stubbed back

wire

strong laterals tied near horizontal

wire

Feathered Maiden on Planting

Year One

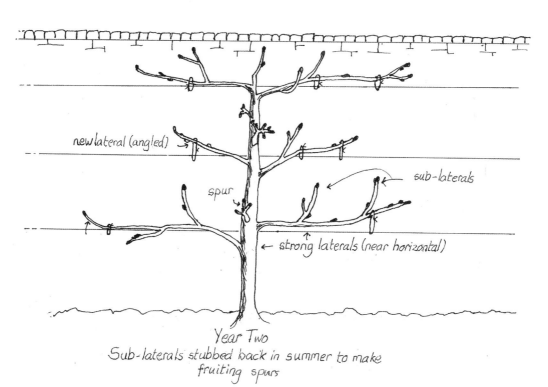

new lateral (angled)

sub-laterals

spur

strong laterals (near horizontal)

Year Two
Sub-laterals stubbed back in summer to make fruiting spurs

First stages in training an espalier.

always working to form each new tier in sequence till the desired height is reached. Never allow the top of the tree to form first, as it will then be next to impossible to achieve that even spacing of branches which makes best use of the wall space.

And never, ever, let the tree carry on growing above the top of the wall, where it will do its own thing out of reach of your interventions! We have seen many small forests laughing down at gardeners from the tops of walls. The head, or tip, will always be the strongest shoot, or collection of shoots, and the trick is to manage this every year by cutting it back to near the top two horizontal branches. Summer-prune most vertical shoots from the horizontals to one or two buds, but cut any strong shoots in the top right out to the main stem. By and large, vertical shoots grow, but they don't bear flowers, or, of course, fruit in their first year. If you leave them, the top of the tree will get heavy, dominant and shade the lower branches, risking disease and fruit that struggles to ripen. The whole espalier is also liable to come away from the wall.

## Fan trees

Making a fan form uses a similar method to creating an espalier. However, only two, four or six branches are selected, then tied in at angles of 45–60 degrees, left and right, on to the wires. All buds and shoots growing into the wall need to be rubbed out and those growing out should be cut back to a stub. Fan training is a better restricted form for plums and cherries, as it restricts the vigour of these species and the fruit benefits from the warmth of a wall.

## Stepovers

These are little trees, single or double-stemmed, for edging borders or raised beds, typically 30–45cm (12–18in) high. To create one, you should ideally start with a tree that has one or two very low branches – the height of the step you want to make. Cut the rest of the tree off above these branches. Tie the two branches on to canes, initially keeping them

An overgrown espalier needing a good prune of its vertical shoots.

slightly upright to encourage growth, but aiming for horizontal, long, stiff branches with lots of fruiting spurs along their length. Install two low wires, along which these branches will be trained.

If your tree has no low branches, you will need to cut the maiden tree down to 20cm (8in) (but make sure that is well above the graft union), forcing new branches in year two. Select the two lowest new branches for training. You may also be able to bend a maiden shoot down without breaking the graft union, if you can curve it down gently and tie it. In both cases, cut back any upright shoots every summer to a 1cm (0.4in) stub, which will form the fruiting spurs.

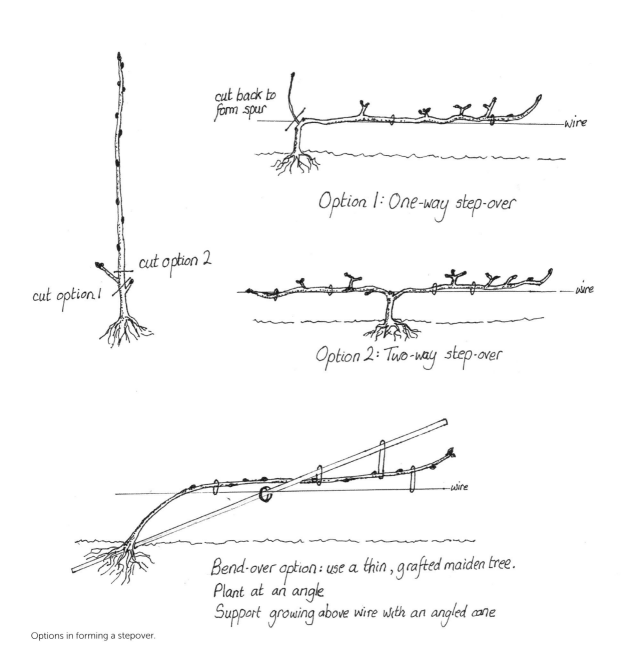

Options in forming a stepover.

After a heavy pruning, this old plum fan is still productive.

Two-stemmed stepover.

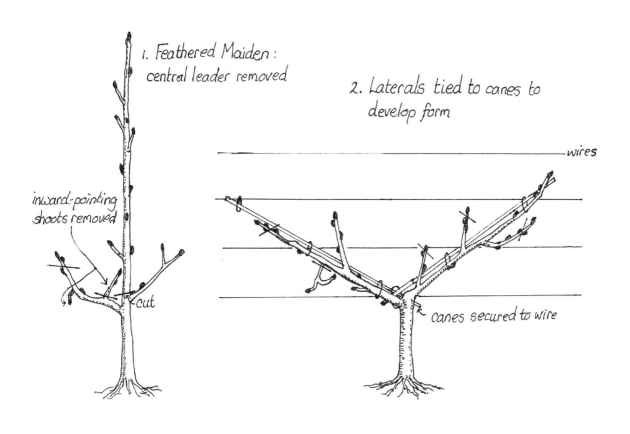

1. Feathered Maiden: central leader removed

2. Laterals tied to canes to develop form

inward-pointing shoots removed

cut

wires

canes secured to wire

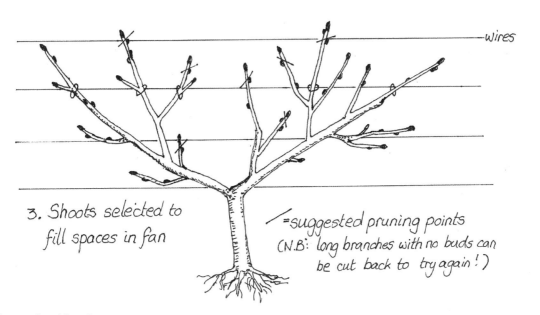

3. Shoots selected to fill spaces in fan

wires

/ = suggested pruning points
(N.B. long branches with no buds can be cut back to try again!)

Early stages in training a fan tree.

## How to train free-standing trees for open spaces

Imagining the future growth of these trees is essential from day one, as, apart from the main trunk, the branches you see then are unlikely to be the ones you will want in the future. The branches that will create the desired shape are yet to form!

It is probable that any branches on the tree supplied by the nursery will be too low down the trunk in the long term. Allow them to bear fruit for a year or two, but plan to remove them, as they will droop to the ground and get in the way of weeding or grass cutting. Branches arising from 1m (3.3ft) up the trunk or higher are potentially valuable, so should be kept. Some varieties, such as the apples Egremont Russet and Ellison's Orange, naturally produce a lot of upright-growing branches. You may need to cut some of these out, while the best placed and strongest will need to be trained to a more horizontal position. This can be achieved by tying down the flexible young growth to a weight or stone on the ground, or to the lower part of the trunk. This is a temporary action – it will be untied as soon as the branch has lignified.

If your new tree has a lot of fussy growth near the top, prune it out to leave one strong leading shoot. If the tree is a 2m (6.6ft) tall maiden showing no sign of branching, cut that leading shoot down to 85–120cm (34–47in) just above a bud immediately after planting.

### Low standard tree

Here, you are aiming for 50–80cm (20–32in) of clear stem before any branches. This allows you to get on the essential rabbit guard and slide the mower underneath in the future. You are also looking to achieve four or five branches radiating from the main stem in all directions.

The buds that break just below the leader tip in spring are likely to be first, but are also most likely to result in a weak, unstable, tight angle between the new branch and the main stem. So, if possible, rub out these two or three buds nearest the top. This will encourage the buds lower down the stem to open and these are more likely to grow horizontally.

If you need to use shoots that are growing upright, they can be tied down temporarily as described above. Hopefully, these initial actions will result in a tree that is wider at the bottom than at the top – a classic cartoon Christmas tree shape – and this will make it easy to achieve a spindle-bush, or pyramid, tree.

### Spindle bush

Commercial orchardists have been producing fruit, especially apples, pears and plums, on the spindle-bush form for a long time now, but it is rarely recommended for amateurs, even though it is very well suited to a small garden situation. Spindle-bush trees, at no more than 3m (10ft) tall, are compact and easy to harvest from and prune. Fruit ripens well from the light being able to reach all parts of the tree. On dwarfing rootstocks, such as M9 or M26 for apples, they crop abundantly and quickly after planting. The close-to-horizontal branches are stronger and better able to take the weight of fruit produced annually. They can be planted as close as 1.5m (5ft) apart, but remember that very dwarf trees trained to this shape need a stake as tall as the tree itself. If serious fruit production is your priority, it is a good idea to learn how to form and prune spindle bushes.

So how is this A-shape achieved and maintained?

- Start with either a well-feathered tree or a tall maiden cut back to 85cm (33.5in), on dwarfing rootstock (M26 or M9 for apples, Quince A for pears).
- Train new branches as they form to near-horizontal, aiming for four to five main-frame branches low on the trunk (between 80 and 120cm [32–47in]).

Maiden tree: no lateral branches yet.

Central leader tree with good feathering.

Two-year-old tree.

Three-year-old apple tree with a double leader.

Avoid double leaders – prune one out.

Stubbed-back double leader.

Prune leaders to a weak branch if the maiden tree is over 1.8m (6ft).

- Keep tipping back the leader while the lower branches are forming.
- Allow thin, short shoots (dards and brindilles) to form on the trunk and the five branches.
- Stub back any thick branches high up on the stem. Only allow thin shoots to persist.
- The trunk should be tied permanently to the post, which should permit the five branches to be tied down to the base of the post to get the initial A-shape framework. The post is needed to hold up the weight of fruit in summer.

## Tip

The best fruit on a spindle bush will be on short, thin, two-year-old wood, not the thick branches.

Tying down branches to the horizontal will help to create a triangular-shaped tree.

From the third year after planting, make sure that you are pruning the top branches hard and the bottom few very little, in order to maintain the triangular A-shape. Take care not to let the top of the tree get too 'busy' with shoots. You also need to encourage a more or less symmetrical, balanced shape, like a cone, with branches spreading to all points of the compass. If you have an uncooperative tree not producing evenly spaced shoots, consider tying the branches around the tree until the wood has hardened and they are pointing the way you want them to. Once your main framework is achieved, it can be left in place unless a branch shows signs of canker or other disease, in which case it should be cut back to the main stem and allowed, by leaving a short stub, to start again.

The spindle-bush method, a commercial success today, is pretty much the opposite to badly managed, mop-headed trees on vigorous rootstocks, where cutting and trimming annually at the top leaves the majority of branches shaded. This results in poor ripening, diseased fruit – and a centre with no fruit at all. Most of the tree's energy goes into growth rather than fruit production, and the poor airflow makes it a target for scab and canker (*see* Chapter 11).

## Follow-on tasks

### Don't forget to untie!

Much of your early pruning and training – as well as the initial planting – will have involved tethering the trees to stakes, canes, wires and heavy weights. It is as important – maybe more so – to untie those knots when the support is no longer needed.

First, you should have the trees tied fairly firmly to the stake, using a double loop. But this must be loosened as the tree grows in girth, otherwise the

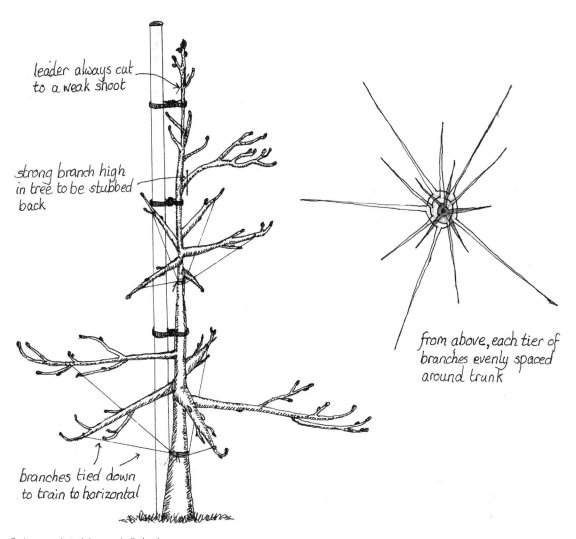

leader always cut
to a weak shoot

strong branch high
in tree to be stubbed
back

from above, each tier of
branches evenly spaced
around trunk

branches tied down
to train to horizontal

Early stages in training a spindle bush.

bark will be damaged and the tree literally strangled as the water and nutrient channels just under the bark are blocked. This is especially important for trees on semi-vigorous or vigorous rootstocks. Tree ties *must* be adjustable and need to be checked annually. Do note, however, that flexible ties for those very dwarf trees are available and it may be possible to leave them in place for the life of the tree.

Likewise, remove training supports such as canes when no longer needed and take off ties harnessing lignified shoots to wires and fences *before* they become branches and try to engulf the neglected ties. You may be tying in new shoots at the same time, which should remind you to liberate branches from ties no longer needed.

One knot we have been guilty of forgetting about in the past is the wire one that holds the label with the tree's name. You need to keep moving any wire hanging labels to thinner branches before the wire cuts in (and probably rewriting the name on as well). Permanent 'in the ground' labels are a safer bet if they are not at risk from vandalism. Scratch-on labels are very durable.

Spindle bushes need a tall stake.

This tree tie is now too tight.

Permanent damage from an overtight tree tie.

Plastic tape is *not* an adjustable tree tie!

Label being eaten by the tree.

## Checking the guards

Whilst checking and loosening ties, routinely check rabbit, deer and vole guards at the end of each winter. Make sure that they are still performing their function and not digging into the tree. Vole guards are fairly rigid and must be removed when the tree is coming up to the diameter of the guard. Spiral guards adjust themselves, being flexible, but a point will be reached when the gaps between the spiralling plastic are so large that there is no longer any point in keeping them in place and, by this time, the plastic is becoming cracked and brittle anyway. If you are removing tree stakes from more vigorous trees, they can be carefully levered out.

## Feeding the trees

During establishment, when the tree roots are still building intense relationships with mycorrhizal fungi

Robust scratch labels.

and finding their way, orchard trees may benefit from some extra nutrition, even in fertile soils.

Phosphorus to encourage root growth can be applied in the form of bonemeal in early spring during the first few years. If growth seems slow, other organic fertilisers (blood, fish and bone, pelletised poultry manure, seaweed meal and so on) also supply nitrogen and many trace elements, and will all give the trees some support, applied as dry granules or pellets. If you choose to use non-organic chemical versions of the above, that's up to you, but remember these are not going to benefit soil fertility, plus habit leads to dependency and overdosing is extremely harmful to the environment. Always stick to the manufacturer's guidelines and don't even dream of throwing in an extra handful for luck!

We would recommend mulching around the tree annually in spring in these early years – garden compost, well-rotted manure, seaweed, leaf mould, spent mushroom compost, straw, wood chippings, or proprietary mulching materials – as this simultaneously feeds in a slow-release form and helps to suppress weed competition, which can set back young trees as they establish. Controlling weeds around the base of the trees is important in the first two years; expect some hand-weeding as well as mulching, but be careful not to damage the all-important surface roots.

Once the trees are expected to start flowering (that could be year one for feathered trees on very dwarfing rootstocks, but for very vigorous rootstocks may not be for another five years or more), you will need to adjust the feed in order to encourage flowering. That means less nitrogen-rich material that favours growth, but a good source of potassium instead. We have a wood-burner and the potash in the cold ashes is all the potassium the trees in our garden get, applied directly around the base whenever the ashcan is emptied. Beware of copying us – in freezing sleet or snow, the apple trees nearest the door get more than their fair share, as we scurry back into the warm as quickly as possible! Well-composted sheep manure or kelp seaweed are other good sources of potassium. The great thing about these forms of potassium is that they are slow-release. There is no rapid flush of nutrients, which could be detrimental, so it is hard to overfeed.

Mulch trees annually.

## Crabs, scrogs and wild fruit trees

There is a lot of confusion about crab apples. First, there is the true native crab apple (*Malus sylvestris*), growing wild in old woods and up hills right across Europe. A true crab-apple tree is a rare find and should be looked after. They are of huge value to wildlife, and especially attractive to pollinators.

Second, there are apple trees growing wild in hedges and field corners, usually near a railway line (active or disused), or a motorway, whose fruit are usually a bit defective, either in size, flavour or general appeal. These are 'wildings' and are usually the result of someone chucking an apple core into the hedge. The seeds in the core will have been cross-pollinated and so grow into trees bearing fruit with little resemblance to the shop-bought Pink Lady or Braeburn they started from. But never disregard a wilding – the genetics sometimes get lucky and a lovely new apple is born – Bramley's Seedling, our best-known cooker, is an example.

Third, there are local names for crab apples, which are sometimes used as a variety name. 'Scrogg' or 'scrog' is one such, used in northern England and the Scottish Borders. Scrog is a generic term for a stunted tree or bush, but when applied to a type of apple tree may or may not produce palatable fruit. It is worth remembering that the sourest crabs were eaten (maybe as cider or cooked as vegetables) before the arrival of the ancestors of our modern varieties.

Local names also are found for the fruit of the wild pear (*Pyrus communis*). Once again, a rare find in the wild, but garden escapes and naturalised pears (*P. pyraster*) can be found. In old, neglected orchards, where the wild pear rootstock has survived the demise of a grafted variety, you'll come across wild pear fruit, round and not pear-shaped, and mistaken easily for stunted apples. Locally to us in eastern Scotland, they are called chokers. With good reason. We tried one once. Only once.

Finally, don't overlook the many splendid cultivars of the wild crab apple, such as Golden Hornet and John Downie, which are intended mainly for ornament, but which make great jellies, wines and cider, as well as luring the bees into the orchard.

Choker pears are not good to eat!

# Blossom Time

## Buds are the key

Buds are the really important part of a fruit tree, yet so often are overlooked. They need to be cherished, guarded against all attackers and removed sometimes for a good reason. For deciduous trees that lose their leaves in winter, most buds are the resting place of next year's leaves. These buds are the key to the growth (and shape) of your tree. Newly unfurling leaves in spring will feed flowers and young fruit, but they are vulnerable at this stage and it is a shame to see them getting frosted in our unpredictable weather patterns. Leaf buds, therefore, are also the key to the number of fruit produced each year. Other fatter, rounder buds contain the flowers themselves. The first one to open is known as the king flower; it will be the one on the end of the cluster. In a poor year, it may only be this one that gets pollinated. Behind this one, there may be five more flowers, which is why we usually get clusters of fruit.

This is a good time to sort out which of your trees are spur-bearers and which are tip-bearers. A branch that has developed clusters of fruiting buds along the length of a branch is a spur-bearer. A tree that has its flowers only from the bud at the end of lots of shoots is a tip-bearer. Look at your plum, pear and apple trees at blossom time to see if there is a clear distinction. Remember, though, that many trees will bear fruit in both ways, tip and spur! A fruiting spur can become very dense and crowded, as new spurs develop on top of the old ones. At blossom time, when flowers start to open, a well-maintained fruit tree is a glorious sight, covered in flowers. The stages in fruit-blossom opening are described as:

The king flower is the first to open.

- **stage one:** mouse-ear
- **stage two:** pink bud
- **stage three:** 80 per cent
- **stage four:** fully open

As the flowers open, nectar and pollen are produced, attracting bees and other pollinators. When the blossom buds are at stages one and two, it is less of a risk to bees and other pollinating insects for non-organic commercial producers to use pesticide and other chemical sprays. Clearly, the risk is severe at stages

Blossom in clusters.

These spurs are set along the branch.

three and four. If you do not intend to spray, you can just have fun identifying and comparing these stages on your different trees. And while having fun, watch those flower buds closely – if aphids move in and suck the sap of newly emerging flowers, this may result in a very poor crop. There will be more information about aphids and how to limit the effects of an infestation in Chapter 10.

Mouse-ear buds.

James Grieve apple at pink-bud stage.

Apple aphids on an unfurling flower.

## What are flowers for?

The energy that a tree expends in producing large, showy and highly scented flowers is only about one thing – attracting insects to carry out pollination. Top fruit trees, our main subjects for discussion, are in the family Rosaceae, whose members are all insect-pollinated. Pollen is produced by the male organs in a flower, called stamens, and brought to ripeness in the anthers, at the top of the flexible stamens. It is worth examining flowers carefully and appreciating their clever structure and beauty.

The stamens will be seen rising among the clustered female organs, called pistils. Anthers vary in colour, some changing as they develop, such as those in pear flowers, which go from red to black. When pollen (the male gametes) is fully developed, the anthers open and pollen is shed. Hopefully, this will be on to the legs or back of a visiting insect, who will then carry it to a different flower, possibly a different tree, where some of it will brush off. Pollen grains are extremely tiny and inevitably some will land on the stigma – the topmost part of the pistil – where they will stick.

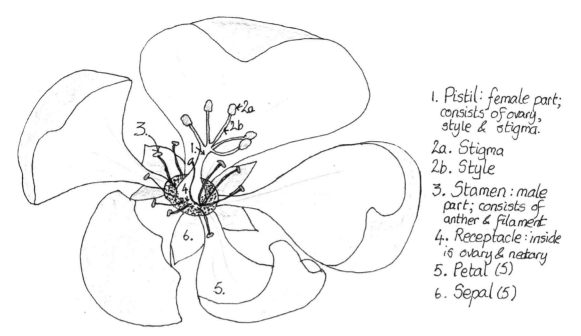

1. Pistil: female part; consists of ovary, style & stigma.
2a. Stigma
2b. Style
3. Stamen: male part; consists of anther & filament
4. Receptacle: inside is ovary & nectary
5. Petal (5)
6. Sepal (5)

Blossom flower structure.

Pollination can be achieved by passing insects.

A race then ensues. What has happened so far is pollination – all well and good. But there will still be no fruit unless grains of pollen unite with ova (female gametes) and the ova are not sitting waiting in the stigma. They are safely in the ovary at the base of the pistil. Between the stigma and the ovary, there is a tube called the style. It varies in length in different types of flowers, but in fruit-tree blossom, especially the stone fruits, it sets a daunting challenge to a pollen grain. Each pollen grain on a stigma must now send a thread of itself down into the style, a thread that grows until it penetrates an ovum. The one that gets there first (the fittest!) will unite with the ovum to make a seed; there is no consolation prize for the rest. This is called fertilisation.

In apples and pears (pip fruit) there are five stigmas, so if all are pollinated and fertilised, there will be five pips inside a fruit. In plums, gages, damsons and cherries (stone fruit) there is one stigma, one ovary and one stone when you eat through the flesh.

You might be wondering why, if flowers contain both male and female gametes (pollen and ova), they don't just fertilise themselves and save themselves

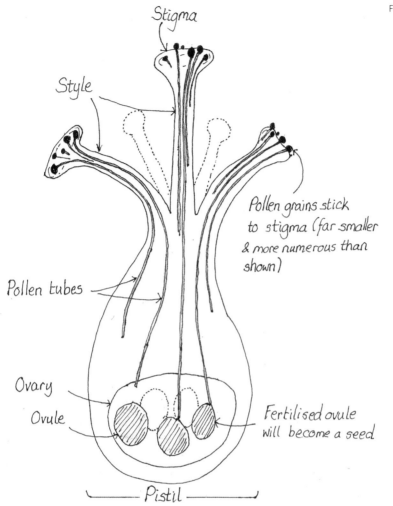

Stigma

Style

Pollen grains stick to stigma (far smaller & more numerous than shown)

Pollen tubes

Ovary

Ovule

Fertilised ovule will become a seed

Pistil

Cherry blossom.

the energy of making beautiful, insect-attracting flowers. In fact, many types of flowers – pea, bean, tomato, for example – do just that and are known as self-pollinating. But there is an advantage for many plants to being cross-pollinated. By encouraging the widest possible gene pool into the population, plants are able to adapt to changing conditions through their offspring, develop resistance to diseases and predation by pests, and many other characteristics. If there is a limited gene pool in the fruit-tree family, it can lead to inbreeding depression, where the population of a species becomes weaker, less successful at reproducing and less healthy.

As well as pollen hitching rides on flying insects to reach other trees and flowers, flowers may be self-incompatible. The pollen may ripen before the stigma (protandry), or vice versa (protogyny). There may be structural or chemical barriers to self-fertilisation. Self-incompatibility (complete or partial) of one kind or another, is fairly common in tree fruit, which is why we recommend having more than one tree of that species nearby. Even if a fruit tree is described as self-fertile, better pollination happens, and therefore more fruit is produced, if some cross-pollination takes place. Yields will be higher and fruit generally of a better quality. Most pollinators will fly a fair way, so the trees do not need to be that close to one another, or even in the same garden or orchard. Many orchardists will incorporate the odd crab apple at the end of a row of apple trees, because crabs flower over a very long period, produce lots of pollen and are capable of cross-pollinating most apple varieties. In our garden, James Grieve apple fulfils much the same purpose.

## What are the best pollinators?

Any insect (or any animal or bird, come to that), which can deliberately or accidentally carry pollen from tree to tree, is a pollinator. Tropical plants may be pollinated by bats or hummingbirds. On trees that have catkins wafting about, the wind does a good job. In China and some other parts of the world where insect pollinators have been decimated, teams of human animals are sent out to orchards to hand-pollinate the fruit trees. If our peach tree decides to flower in a very cold snap that keeps the bumblebees snuggled up, we go in with a feather or soft brush.

In Britain, insect pollination is by far the most important method. According to the charity Buglife (the Invertebrate Conservation Trust), one in three of every mouthful of food we eat is dependent on insect pollination. With apples, plums and pears, that goes up to probably 100 per cent! That is why insects and other invertebrates are so vital and need our protection, not regular annihilation by pesticides.

Peaches come into flower in February.

Top of the pollinator achievement charts are the bees. The British Beekeepers' Association[5] tells us that there are around 24 species of bumblebee and over 240 species of solitary bee in Britain, as well as domesticated and feral colonies of *Apis mellifera* – the honeybee. Bees are ectotherms, that is, their body temperature depends largely on the external environment and different species have differing thresholds at which it becomes possible to get the thoracic flight muscles working, so it is important to look after *all* of our pollinators. In cold weather, solitary bees or bumblebees may be the only ones out working. But on warm, still days in spring when the sun is out, they will all be seen in numbers, moving from flower to flower.

Most, if not all, bees are important pollinators. As a rule, the more furry the insect's body, the more readily it picks up pollen. Honeybees, being social insects, have many larvae at home waiting to be fed and as they eat pollen (a vital source of protein for the growing larvae), honeybees will be seen with bulging pollen sacs on their kneecaps. Far from being detrimental to pollination, though, the foraging honeybee simply cannot help but carry more pollen on her back, abdomen and hairy legs, most of which will be abandoned on the stigma of one of the next flowers visited.

Orchard flowers, in common with most, have evolved to produce nectar. As far as anyone knows, the effort that a plant puts into nectar production is purely to attract insects like bees, for whom it is energy-giving food (converted by bees into honey and stored). The nectary is usually hidden deep within a flower and to reach it an insect has to brush past the pollen-laden anthers – so, once again, they are obliged to pollinate.

Bee species vary in the ways that they forage. Bumblebees and other solitary bees tend to go from tree to tree haphazardly, which probably makes them more effective overall at cross-pollination than honeybees. A common question we are asked is whether apples cross-pollinated by a different variety give a hybrid fruit, for example something between a Bramley and a Cox. The answer is no – regardless of where the pollen came from, the apples on a Bramley will always be Bramleys, on a Cox's Orange Pippin, they will be Cox's Orange Pippin apples and so on. But the seeds inside will be genetically varied and may possibly produce horrid-tasting fruit, which, again, is why fruit trees are grafted.

Honeybees are generally faithful to one type of flower when out foraging – behaviour which is famously choreographed by the various waggle dances foragers perform when they get home with

Cherry-plum flower hoping for early bumble or solitary bees.

pollen or nectar. So, if they start on apple blossom, they will continue on apple blossom, till a scout bee comes in with a better idea. But, being methodical creatures, honeybees in a nice, neat, gridiron orchard will also tend to move in one direction up a row. That means they might get distracted by a field of spring rape before doing all the rows and, as they would prefer to fly in the direction of the wind, the trees in the west end of the row might not get full pollination. The scout bees will be distracted by any crop that

looks more promising than your fruit trees, so don't be surprised when the dandelions are out to find far more honeybees busy in the grass than in the tree blossom. Conversely, if your orchard is the shining light of forage in a barren wilderness of sprayed verges and cereal crops, honeybees will fly 5km (3 miles) or more just to visit.

As cross-pollination is so important to the fruit grower, it is unsurprising that many of us have a hive or two of honeybees in the garden, or play host to a commercial beekeeper with many more. Given the fact that honeybees don't get up particularly early and won't go out to forage at all if it's too wet, cold or windy, it is estimated that for every hectare of orchard, you would need around two and a half healthy honeybee colonies at blossom time to pollinate apple trees, maybe more for pears – if there were no other pollinators. Orchards and bees go hand in hand, but do not go into beekeeping lightly. Join a local group, chain yourself to a knowledgeable beekeeper on his rounds, read up and be prepared. It is a great, absorbing and rewarding occupation, but it carries responsibilities and risks. If you do have hives in the orchard, keep the numbers up in spring to cover all pollination eventualities.

## Other pollinators

Given the more random foraging visits of bumblebees and their ability to carry on working in inclement weather and for much longer hours than honeybees, you might want to think of ways to support and encourage bumble and other wild bees, rather than keeping honeybees. The white-tailed, early and buff-tailed bumblebees (*Bombus lucorum*, *B. pratorum* and *B. terrestris*) all work quicker than honeybees on fruit trees and you can easily construct or purchase 'bumblebee houses' to accommodate them. Our approach has always been to make sure that the garden or orchard has a wide range of habitats for the widest range of species, to never be too neat and tidy, and to tolerate – no, to enjoy – our native invertebrate pollinator population wherever it takes up residence. This includes turning a blind eye to the odd wasp byke if it's not putting anyone in danger, as wasps are good, effective pollinators and will vacate the nest or byke in September anyway, as only the new queens survive by hibernating for winter. Buff-tailed bumblebees may nest in the rockery, so what? Solitary mining bees such as *Andrena* – great little pollinators – make colonies under the lawn ... what else is a lawn for?

Other species known to pollinate orchard blossom include hoverflies, fluffy bee-flies, leafcutter bees and even hairy blowflies. In those years when winter drags its feet and spring is cold and late, there may not even be many bumblebees working when early blossom – such as cherry-plum and peach – comes out. Then we rely on all these other insect pollinators to ensure crop pollination, many of whom are also predators of common orchard pests, as we will see in Chapter 10. They need from us places to hibernate as well as places to breed and it is easy

DIY wild bee nest boxes.

Flowers under the trees will help to attract pollinating insects.

Orchard Management
The grass in the orchard is cut as a hay meadow in mid-July. This ensures a good display of narcissi and snakeshead fritillaries each Spring. Autumn crocus will follow in September/October.

Hay meadows are good habitats for orchard invertebrates.

to build your own bug hotel using waste materials such as broken garden canes, bundles of straw, hollow stems (sunflowers are good), broken bricks (the types with holes in), corrugated cardboard, a bit of shelter and imagination. A bit of wilderness and wet in the garden goes a long way towards good pollination, as does variety of habitat, understanding and love of nature.

As well as habitat, pollinators will need plenty of forage crops to keep them thriving when the orchard is not in flower. One of the most strictly managed commercial orchards we know is nevertheless surrounded on two sides by wide swathes of wildflower and bee-friendly plants, such as *Phacelia tanacetifolia*. Apart from our native wildflowers, bees are particularly attracted to members of the borage family

## Key insect pollinators of fruit trees

Many, mostly flying, insects are attracted to the rich nectar of fruit-tree blossom and any found on a flower can technically pollinate. But some are better than others, such as those for whom nectar or pollen are an essential food source and those with hairy bodies or legs to which pollen grains will stick. Plus, of course, those that are out and about when fruit trees are in flower. Here are some of the best.

**Social insects (living in colonies)**
- Honeybee (*Apis mellifera*)

- All bumblebees and carder bees (*Bombus* spp.)
- Wasps (*Vespa* spp.)

**Solitary bees (living as individuals but often with many others of the same species in close proximity)**
- Mining bees (*Andrena* spp.)
- Mason bees (*Osmia* spp.)
- Leafcutter bees (*Megachile cetuncularis*)
- Cuckoo bees (*Psithyrus* spp.) – which lay their eggs in the nests of bumblebees

**Flies**
- Hoverflies (Family *Syrphidae*)
- Bee flies (*Bombylius* spp.)

(especially borage itself, alkanet and all the comfreys), the geranium family, the thistle family (some lovely ornamentals in this group, but the globe thistle reigns supreme here for numbers of pollinators on one flower), the daisy family (bumblebees and hoverflies love sunflowers) and some of the pea family. The deadnettle family deserves special mention, as not only does it contain lovely ornamentals such as *Stachys macrantha*, lamb's lugs (*Stachus byzantina*) and betony (*Stachys officinalis*), it also contains the great majority of garden herbs, from lavender and rosemary to marjoram, hyssop, sage and all the thymes. You could do a lot worse than plant herbs near your fruit trees – it works for us!

You may be wondering how the nasty pests are kept out – isn't all this habitat and forage going to attract pests as well? The short answer is, quite likely. If you want to help pollinators, there are bound to be some you don't like. You can't put up no entry signs or demand that invertebrates show a valid visa. But by providing a range of habitats and strategies as simple as keeping some grass short and some longer, you will also attract predators – insect, spider, bird and mammalian ones – who are part of the picture of keeping pests under control. There is more about natural predators and keeping the balance in Chapters 10 and 12.

Sunflowers are much loved by bees and hoverflies.

## Pollinisers and pollination groups

As we have seen, even self-fertile fruit trees will get better fruit set and higher yields if they are cross-pollinated. The orchardist or fruit-tree gardener will want to be sure that there are other fruit trees close by and in flower at roughly the same time for the pollinators to work on.

### Apples

Trees that are a compatible source of pollen for other trees are known as pollinisers. Some are very good at it, producing a superabundance of pollen over a long period, such as the crab apples for pollinating apple varieties. Many very ornamental crab apples are tried and tested pollinisers and if you have room for more than one, plant different varieties. There are also apple varieties that flower for a long time, like James Grieve, and ones that produce lots of pollen, like Golden Delicious.

The Royal Horticultural Society[6] lists seven different pollination groups for apples and it is easy to get very worried about having the right pollinisers. However, a closer look will reveal that the vast majority of varieties are in Flowering Groups 2, 3 and 4 – the 'mid-season' flowerers. Not only do the trees in these groups all pollinate each other, most Group 2 trees will pollinate Group 1 and most of Group 4 will pollinate Group 5. Keep in mind that apple varieties will flower in a specific date order – being in the same artificial pollination group does *not* mean two trees will flower on the same day. Many catalogues and nurseries will provide polliniser information based on flowering date order and it is perhaps more useful to know the date order than the group. But remember, too, that there are no clear cut-off points and apple trees are usually in flower for three weeks or more. A six-day overlap in flowering dates is considered enough for pollination to be effective.

Worcester Pearmain apples – one of the last to flower in our garden.

'Golden Hornet' is a beautiful crab apple for pollination.

We would recommend that you think more in terms of early, mid- and late season flowerers and do not be too concerned unless you know you have an early or a late in the mix, with no crab apples to sort out the problem. From mid-April to mid-May, all your apple trees will flower for three weeks each. The earlies will pollinate the mid-seasons, while the mid-seasons will pollinate the lates. In our own garden, the very late-flowering Court Pendu Plat is the only apple tree we have not persuaded to bear fruit and this is because all our other varieties are early or mid-season. Even James Grieve has failed to oblige!

If you live in a town or populated area, your trees will also have access to all the pollen in neighbouring plots and gardens. You are not looking for 100 per cent pollination – try counting all the flowers on your tree and consider what a massive crop of apples you would have to deal with if they all became fruit. Apple trees,

## Table 3: Simple listing of pollination groups for popular apples

| Early flowering | Mid-season flowering | Late flowering |
|---|---|---|
| Adam's Pearmain | Annie Elizabeth | American Mother |
| Alkmene | Ashmead's Kernel | Court Pendu Plat |
| Arbroath Pippin (Oslin) | Beauty of Moray | Crawley Beauty |
| Arthur Turner | Bloody Ploughman | Edward VII |
| Beauty of Bath | Bramley | Newton Wonder |
| Belle de Boskoop | Cambusnethan Pippin | Royal Jubilee |
| Clydeside | Catshead | Suntan |
| Coul Blush | Charles Ross | |
| Devonshire Quarrendon | Cox Pomona | |
| Early Julyan | Discovery | |
| Egremont Russet | Ellison's Orange | |
| Greensleeves | Falstaff | |
| Keswick Codlin | Galloway Pippin | |
| Lass o' Gowrie | Grenadier | |
| Laxton's Fortune | Hawthornden | |
| Mank's Codlin | Hood's Supreme | |
| Monarch | James Grieve | |
| Newton Wonder | Jupiter | |
| Port Allen Russet | Katy | |
| Quinte | Laxton's Superb | |
| Red Devil | Liberty | |
| Ribston Pippin | Saturn | |
| Saint Edmund's Pippin | Scots Bridget | |
| Scotch Dumpling | Stirling Castle | |
| Stobo Castle | Sunset | |
| Tower of Glamis | Winter Gem | |
| | Worcester Pearmain | |

like most plants, overproduce flowers, otherwise we would be overrun with cider and apple sauce.

Table 3 does not list every variety you may come across. Some other apple varieties, you need to be aware, may present particular issues for pollination. They have been bred to contain an extra set of chromosomes in their genetic make-up. These varieties are known as triploid and the big advantage they have is usually in the size of the fruit. Several popular varieties are triploid, such as Bramley, Ribston Pippin, Belle de Boskoop and Ashmead's Kernel. However, they will produce very little pollen and will not be able to pollinate either themselves or any other tree. Therefore, if you have only two trees and one is triploid, the second has to be self-fertile and has the job of pollinating both the triploid and itself. If you have three, the other two can be self-infertile, but only if they all overlap in flowering time. You won't get fruit at all from a glorious orchard of a dozen trees if they are all triploid! So always check if the tree you are buying is triploid and plan accordingly if there are few or no other apple trees in your vicinity. Our Belle de Boskoop is well served with pollinisers and crops well as a cordon – you'd never guess it had a genetic problem!

Less of an issue for small-scale or amateur orchardists – for now – is cross-incompatibility, which arises from the overuse of the same few varieties in breeding programmes. Basically, the number of trees some varieties are capable of pollinating is reduced. If you desired an orchard consisting of only one or two of the compromised varieties – for example, Braeburn – you could expect a pretty poor crop. There is much to be said for growing as wide a range of varieties as your orchard can accommodate.

Following is a list of good polliniser crab-apple varieties. These beautiful, long-flowering crab apples will decorate your orchard and take care of most pollination – and remember that the fruit also has culinary uses.

- *Malus* 'Evereste' – a profusion of flowers over a long period

- *Malus* 'Golden Hornet' – blossom followed by attractive and usable golden crabs in autumn
- *Malus* 'Aldenhamensis' – purple-leafed crab, with dark red blossom
- *Malus* 'John Downie' – excellent for large crab apples for preserves
- *Malus* 'Hillieri' – beautiful pink and white blossom, a later flowerer

## Plums, damsons and gages

This group can be quite confusing, as requirements for pollination and a decent crop of fruit vary a good deal. If you are planting plums, it is worth doing the research on the variety you wish to grow and making sure that any necessary polliniser trees are in the vicinity.

First, there are fully self-compatible varieties. These will set and develop a full crop with their own

Crab apple John Downie is a good polliniser.

pollen. Into this group come all the cherry-plums (also known as myrobalan plums), which are all diploid (no extra sets of chromosomes to worry about). Cultivated Bullace will also self-pollinate. Fortunately, many of the most popular plums in the UK are self-compatible too: Victoria, Marjorie's Seedling, Czar, Jubilee, River's Early Prolific, both Purple and Yellow Pershore plums and the delightfully named Warwickshire Drooper. Also self-compatible is the only commercially available Scottish plum, Gordon Castle. Among the damsons, Merryweather and Shropshire Prune will self-pollinate and give a good crop with no pollinisers nearby. Gages are a group known as poor self-pollinators, but one exception is Denniston's Gage. Ouillins and Early Transparent gages should also be expected to crop well through self-pollination.

Second, there are varieties that are partially self-compatible, but which set a pretty poor crop unless there is some cross-pollination as well. Cambridge Gage and Farleigh Damson, both excellent varieties, will require at least one other tree to achieve a good crop. Ouillins Gage and Merryweather or Shropshire Prune damsons should do the job. Early flowering plums such as Avalon, Utility, Haganta or Curlew will benefit from an input of pollen from Reine-Claude de Bavay or Warwickshire Drooper. The very popular mid-season plums River's Early, Opal, Jubilee and Early Laxton are also partially self-incompatible – squeeze in a Czar or a Stanley, or borrow a neighbour's Victoria to ensure good crops on these.

The third group, which include delectable plums such as Jefferson, Coe's Golden, Excaliber, Kirke's Blue, President, Valor, Reeves and Sanctus Hubertus, as well as the iconic Old Green Gage, are fully non-self-compatible (also described as self-sterile). They will not set fruit from their own pollen, so polliniser trees must be present. Choose pollinisers that are in peak flower at the same time, where possible. Most plums, gages and damsons flower over a twenty-day period, but peak at different times.

Finally, there are plums about which there is insufficient knowledge of how they are pollinated. If you have one of these unclassified trees, it is best to assume that it will need a polliniser or two. You may need to know about the few varieties that are cross-incompatible as well, that is, they will pollinate anything but each other. They are not commonly sold, but you may inherit one when taking over a garden, so it is worth checking if you consistently get no fruit. There are some curious cross-pollination incidents – Old Green Gage which will not pollinate itself, is very good at pollinating the self-sterile President, as will Cambridge Gage. On a final note, if in doubt, plant a Mirabelle cherry-plum!

## Pears

Everything said above about apples pretty much also applies to pears. With the opportunity for

Some greengages are self-pollinating.

Cherry-plum flowers are tough and self-fertile.

cross-pollination, you will almost always get a better crop than with a single tree. That said, there are varieties that will self-pollinate reasonably successfully, including the most popular varieties – Concorde and Conference, and, to an extent, Williams Bon Chretien. These are also the easiest trees to get hold of.

The mid-season flowering pears will be capable of pollinating other pears in their group, plus nearly all the early and late varieties. Williams Bon Chretien, Beth and Glou Morceau are good examples, plus Winter Nelis for a tasty late fruit. From the point of view of being polliniser trees, Beurre Hardy and Merton Pride are poor choices, the latter being a triploid tree bearing little pollen. Jargonelle is another triploid, accepting and needing, but not delivering, useful amounts of pollen.

Late-flowering pears include Comice, the striking Humbug, Onward and Invincible. Concorde is also in this group. You will need another late to pollinate the very late-flowering Hellen's Early (it's the fruit that's the early part) and you may have trouble getting fruit from triploid pear Louise Bonne of Jersey, which flowers very early indeed, if you only have pears from the late group. We have one that has never made fruit in ten years!

## Other fruit trees

There are many reliably self-fertile modern cherries, including Stella and Morello. Some older varieties, though, are self-sterile. These include Van, Early Rivers and Merton Glory, so do not choose these if you have room for only one cherry. Consult your local nursery for more information.

Quinces and medlars are useful fruit trees in the orchard, but few households would need more than one. Fortunately, Quinces Vranja, Aromatnaya,

Cherry blossom is no guarantee of fruit – you may need a polliniser, too.

Quince makes a lovely small tree.

Medlars are an unusual fruit, which are easy to grow.

Isfahan, Meech's Prolific and Serbian Gold are all reliably self-compatible, as is Medlar Nottingham.

## Still no fruit?

If there is still no fruit, what has gone wrong? The most likely cause is the weather. Weather affects not only the blossom, but the trees themselves. Low temperatures in autumn can prevent blossom buds from ripening, while wind, rain and drought can all damage flowers. Weather also greatly affects the actions of pollinators.

Some fruit trees, such as cherry-plum and pears, come into flower very early in spring and our weather in Britain does not guarantee ideal conditions for pollinators to be out and about. As ectotherms, bees need the outside temperature to reach a certain point before they are physically able to fly. You will see them taking nectar from snowdrops and early crocuses on sunny days (one reason to have a honeybee hive entrance facing the morning sun is to get them up early), but successive days of heavy frost will call a halt to all pollination. Other insects may be more cold-tolerant, but are less effective at pollination, or might be around in much lower numbers. Bees also really hate having to fly in strong winds and will skulk in their beds if there's a gale blowing.

Frost not only keeps insects in bed, it will also have a detrimental effect on the blossom itself. Even when pollinated, the growth of the pollen tube is slower in cold conditions and fertilisation won't happen. In 2021 in eastern Scotland, when heavy frosts persisted from late April to the middle of May, we expected any blossom opening then, or most newly formed fruitlets, to be physically damaged by the frost. Curiously, though, we found that the trees that had blossomed earlier and set fruit in the unusually warm late March and April kept their fruit and we had reasonable crops from them. So set fruit is less vulnerable than blossom to frost damage. In other parts of the country, where frost came earlier, people only got crops from their late-flowering trees. Sometimes, those at higher altitudes or more northerly latitudes will achieve a decent yield, because, although the order in which fruit trees blossom does not change, these places had enough delay to the start of flowering to miss the frosts.

With our weather conditions, unpredictable at the best of times, thrown into chaos by climate change, our orchards may be increasingly challenged. What can we do? We would advise:

- Don't put all your eggs in one basket. Combine different fruit species and different varieties from early to late. That way, you should always get some harvest.

- Use walls and other shelter to create the warmth that beats the freeze – pears here in eastern Scotland did especially well against walls in 2021 when we had severe frosts in mid-May.
- Do not give up on trees that produce poorly one year. Often, they will overcompensate the following year and from then on produce well every other year, being too exhausted in the years between. This is called biennialism, or biennial bearing. While it can be frustrating, it can also become an advantage – so long as all your trees don't have the same 'off' year!

Durondeau pear benefits from the warmth of a south-facing wall.

## Fruit trees that challenge pollination

For these very early flowering apple varieties, make sure that they have at least one other early to pollinate them:

- Arbroath Pippin (Oslin)
- Clydeside
- Keswick Codlin
- Mank's Codlin
- Port Allen Russet
- Red Astrachan
- Scots Dumpling.

You will also need to ensure partners for these very late-flowering apple varieties:

- Edward VII
- Court Pendu Plat
- Crawley Beauty
- Royal Jubilee.

Triploid trees must have two polliniser partners in the vicinity. They include these apples:

- Belle de Boskoop
- Bramley
- Blenheim Orange
- Gravenstein
- Jupiter
- Reinette du Canada
- Ribston Pippin
- Warner's King.

And these pears:

- Catillac
- Jargonelle
- Louise Bonne of Jersey.

## Apple Days and Blossom Days

In England and Wales, Apple Day has been set, semi-officially, as 21 October, purely because the first 'National Apple Day', in 1990, was held on that date. There are no hard and fast rules. Most Apple Days are organised by community groups and centre around either a community orchard or an old local orchard, and therefore a weekend is chosen for when most people are available

We get to go to a lot of Apple Days in Scotland, from the Clyde Valley to Glasgow City to the shores of Loch Leven and, of course, our own historic Carse of Gowrie orchards. They mostly all feature a cider press, giving people the chance to press their own apple glut. Groups tend to go for the end of October, when most apples are in – but, in reality, it actually depends on how organised people are in reserving the hire of a cider press! So, Apple Days can be every weekend from early September to mid-November.

Pressing apples, drinking the juice, or, for the grown-ups, last year's cider, all go down well. It's always rewarding to see the look of amazement and hear the Oliver Twist pleas for 'more' from suspicious kids trying the sludgy brown fresh juice for the first time. Also popular are apple identification, printmaking and other craft work, apple baking competitions and orchard tours.

Walking through an orchard, though, is even better at blossom time – it's magical. Keeping a community connected with its local orchards is one reason to hold an annual Blossom Day as well as the harvest celebration. It's something local beekeepers like to get involved in and a demonstration hive is a magnetic draw. Orchard tours to point out the stages of blossom, the forms of both fruit blossom and all the other orchard flowers, plus picnics under the trees, all help people to understand the vital link between insects and fruit via pollination. And, of course, a Blossom Day isn't exclusive to apples!

## Chapter Seven

# The Orchard in Summer

The orchard in summer probably conjures up pictures of hammocks and picnics under laden branches, as you lazily watch the fruits of your (and the bees') labour swell and ripen. Well, there is all that … but, also, some moderately relaxed tasks that you should not overlook if you want a healthy and productive orchard. In this chapter, we will therefore cover what you need to know about:

- pruning stone fruit (plums, cherries and so on)
- summer pruning of pip fruit (apples, pears and so on)
- managing the growing crop
- the start of ripening
- other summer tasks to ensure healthy trees and fruit

## Pruning stone fruit

There are good reasons to never prune plums, damsons, peaches, apricots and cherries in winter. The main ones are diseases called silverleaf and bacterial canker (*see* Chapter 11), which thrive and spread in wet autumns and winters, entering any wound (pruning or otherwise) on these types of fruit tree. In fact, bacterial canker will spread in any wet conditions, so check the weather forecast before you begin – even in June! The risk is lower in summer, not just because of weather and being largely outside fungal spore-production season, but also because tree wounds heal more quickly then.

### Plums, damsons, cherry-plums, gages

You can see from the above that it is best to keep the amount of pruning of these trees to a minimum. You also want to avoid accidental wounds from, for example, branches overladen with plums breaking off under the weight of fruit. This is a common occurrence, partly because people are unsure when, whether or how to prune plums, and partly because it's too easy to underestimate how heavy those branches are going to be when the fruit is full sized – we just don't notice in time. Plums are vigorous and the best rootstocks are only semi-dwarfing, so they are nearly always going to need some work. We would never advise pruning plums unnecessarily, but keep in mind these important precepts:

- Keep the tree open, with good airflow, and branches spaced evenly around the tree, as congestion breeds disease.
- Do not encourage or allow the branches to grow year on year, so that they become long and spindly – try to maintain short, sturdy branches for fruit bearing. This also reduces the urge of a plum tree to throw out masses of vigorous, non-fruiting 'water shoots'.
- Make sure that dead, dying or diseased wood is taken out, especially on the small branches that have been shaded on the underside of the tree – sometimes this is easier to spot in summer.
- In older trees, work out what shape the tree's original framework was and try to restore it

to that, with no water shoots, unbalanced or overlong branches.

- Aim for many short, fruiting shoots, coming from only four or five main branches. However, do remove some shoots if they become crowded. Keep in mind that thin shoots may offer the best fruiting wood.

These are our recommendations for tackling plum-pruning, which assume a certain level of hesitancy or neglect in preceding seasons! For example, most established plum trees have formed a round-headed mop, optimistically named a 'bush', on a single stem, because plums are not easy to form into open-centred trees (they will respond by throwing a mass of water shoots into the centre, which is no longer 'open' by any stretch of the imagination).

Better if you can train the central leader using a tall stake from the start and prune the tree to form a pyramid – a bit like an apple spindle bush (described

Unpruned plum trees often become a tangle of branches.

Open-grown young plum tree.

Water shoots often arise from a pruning wound in the centre of the tree.

in Chapter 5). The upper branches are pruned harder than the lower ones; the lowest branch can be quite low on the trunk, as it won't be getting shaded by the upper ones.

However, if the tree is already forming an open centre from the nursery, or has been trained like that for a few years, then continue to keep the centre open. Leave only short shoots and shorten all the main branches. Remember to:

- Cut back hard the long arching shoots in the top of tree that give it a 'weeping' appearance. These will otherwise shade everything below.
- Balance the tree by cutting back the longest branches.
- Cut back all new growth on secondary branches to reduce congestion.
- Deal with any water shoots in the middle of the tree. Only keep them if the tree is in poor condition and they can be trained to replace diseased or dead branches.
- Take off any broken branches. (These are especially common in Victoria plums.)
- Remove any suckers arising from low on the trunk.
- Tip any shoots that are so low as to get in the way of mowing.
- Take off any diseased or dried-up fruit that are hanging over from last autumn.
- Throughout, keep pruning tools clean to avoid transferring disease from tree to tree.

The weight of the crop often leads to broken branches on plums.

If this is an established but neglected tree, you will probably get a lot of vigorous regrowth from this first pruning and will need to work on reducing this every year. Eventually, the tree will be balanced between fruiting and a small amount of growth. Plum trees can get unmanageably tall, especially if they become taller than your long-armed pruners! The rootstock may be against you – Brompton or even St Julien rootstocks will try to grow taller than this – and you will need to reduce the tops at least every two years to keep them to a workable height. Don't hesitate to cut back a trunk to lower replacement shoots if it is showing dead areas higher up.

## Getting the timing right

We know. We do understand how painful it is to prune away a branch laden with ripening fruit. It goes against the grain, but sometimes, with the plum family, you may have to. If you have one of those poor, overburdened, tangled mop-head trees, it must be done while the tree is in growth; delaying till September when you may have picked the fruit isn't an option. Late July or August will be far better and may avoid some of those accidentally broken branches as well. Just grit your teeth – focus on getting those sturdy branches and open centres.

With peaches, apricots and most cherries (especially if under cover), the problem doesn't arise, as the fruit ripens obligingly early and you can prune them afterwards in most cases – July or August for peaches, nectarines and apricots, depending on whether they are grown under cover. You may also be lucky with cherry-plums or mirabelles, which start to ripen in August.

## Cherries

Most cherries can be pruned as soon as the fruit is off. Dwarf cherry trees on Gisela rootstock are not likely

A typical badly pruned
mop-headed plum.

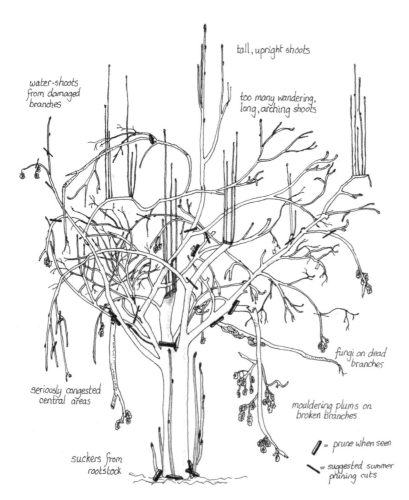

tall, upright shoots

water-shoots
from damaged
branches

too many wandering,
long, arching shoots

fungi on dead
branches

seriously congested
central areas

mouldering plums on
broken branches

⎮ = prune when seen

╱ = suggested summer
pruning cuts

suckers from
rootstock

The sort of mess that comes from failing
to summer-prune a plum tree.

How this tree could look after remedial pruning.

to have too much growth to remove, but do thin out crowded shoots and tie down the remaining shoots where this is needed to make them more horizontal (and thus more likely to bear crops). Cut out any diseased or damaged shoots. Cherries on vigorous rootstocks are more likely to get out of control and may need to have branches cut back to the main stem. This can usually be done using long-armed pruning tools. Be sure to remove the quick-growing, vertical water shoots and reduce any especially long branches to balance the tree.

If you are growing acid or cooking cherries, be aware that they flower and fruit on the previous year's wood. (If you are not sure whether a tree is an acid or a sweet cherry, checking the location of flowers and

fruit will identify the type.) They need to be tipped back regularly.

## Summer pruning of pip fruit

Some very vigorous apple varieties, such as Bramley, need to be pruned in summer, as otherwise they will put out a mass of regrowth in spring after standard winter pruning and become too crowded and disease-prone. Cut all new, current season's growth back to two or three buds. This will encourage them to produce more fruit and less growth wood each year. Bramley is one of a number of fruit varieties that are triploid (having an extra set of

Nice open-centred cherry tree.

chromosomes); this is what makes it especially vigorous. Treat other triploid varieties, as well as any other trees that are particularly vigorous, in the same way.

Pruning is focused on getting more of the wood on which flowers are borne. This varies with each variety, so observe where flowering takes place. The flowering shoots – spurs and dards – may be borne on one-, two- or three-year-old wood. Some varieties, such as the apple Sunset, produce a lot of spurs all along their branches, so aim to produce a strong framework of lateral branches starting at 80cm to 1m high (32–39in). Sublateral shoots with fruiting spurs will arise from these, and a proportion can be cut back to stubs in rotation (some, but not all, each year) to give fresh young shoots.

Other varieties, such as Worcester Pearmain apples, flower and fruit mostly on the tips of short branches and are known as 'tip-bearers'. The more tips you have, the more apples. So, the sublaterals in this case must be allowed to become dards and brindilles, allowing flower clusters on the end of the short shoots. Every few years, cut back some of these short shoots to a few centimetres from the main branch, leaving a short stub, and allow new shoots to appear, in rotation as above.

Open-grown, vigorous Bramley apple trees will benefit from summer pruning.

These apples have formed from fruiting spurs and dards.

Bare wood is a feature of tip-bearing Worcester Pearmains.

Most summer pruning of pip fruit, however, is carried out on restricted forms such as cordons, fans and espaliers. Cut away vertical shoots, and other current year's growth, back to a stub, or an existing fruit cluster. The stub will form more fruit buds in the future. Removing this growth takes away leaves that would otherwise be shading the fruit, thereby encouraging ripening. Remove shoots heading into the wall or fence, too. At the same time as pruning, gently tie in the growing leaders of fan and espalier trees against fences or walls, as well as the leaders of young spindle-bush trees to their tall posts.

Good summer pruning of restricted-form apples and pears often means that there is very little pruning to do on these trees in winter. But if you find that your summer pruning has led to lots of soft growth likely to be damaged by the winter frosts, you have gone into summer too early! Delay next year until August, or even early September. The 'right' time will vary across the country.

## Managing the growing crop

The number of flowers pollinated, if all grew into fruit, would be far more than a tree could service in terms of nutrition, support and ripening space. Therefore, it is quite normal for a percentage of small-formed fruit to drop off a tree, thinning the fruit clusters. This is called the 'June drop', although it frequently doesn't

Espalier needing a few vertical summer shoots pruned off.

happen until July! The fruit that drop will usually be incompletely pollinated (these are often a different colour from the fully pollinated ones), together with diseased or infested fruit, which must be swept up and disposed of away from the orchard. Hot, dry summer weather can also cause fruit to drop off, so make sure that you throw a bucket of water over the base of each tree if we get a good summer!

If, after sweeping up the June drop, you find there are still masses of fruit on any one tree, or clusters of four, five, six or more fruit rubbing against one another, consider thinning them out. This can be especially important with plums, as it's very easy for immature green plums to hide unnoticed until they start to change colour in late summer or early autumn, by which time some heavily laden branches may have collapsed and broken. Be sure to thin heavy fruit clusters at the ends of thin branches, as these will be the first to snap.

Trying to bring too many fruit to ripeness puts a strain on a tree, leading to mineral deficiencies causing disorders such as bitter pit in apples (*see* Chapter 11), as well as small, distorted fruit and general poor health. Many trees, if they 'overbear' one year, will produce nothing the following year, setting a pattern of biennial bearing.

By June, you should be able to start thinning the young fruit by pinching them out between your finger and thumb, Later, as the fruit is larger, you should

This cluster of immature plums will need thinning out.

use narrow-bladed secateurs. Take off any dead or dying fruitlets first, then aim to reduce clusters to no more than two or three at most. If there is plenty of fruit on the tree, aim for the space of a fist between each one.

The weight of too much fruit can destroy the shape of a tree.

## The start of ripening

Cherries will be ready to pick in summer. However, if you want any cherries at all to reach your plate, you will need to protect them by netting very thoroughly in June. If you don't, blackbirds will have the lot and they know fine well about getting in under the netting if you don't peg it down. Incidentally, this is why cherries really have to be on dwarf rootstocks, so that they can be grown in fruit cages or net tunnels.

Peaches and figs will ripen in summer and you should frequently give the fruit a very gentle squeeze – if the flesh gives at all, pick and eat! With peaches, the smell of ripe fruit is a helpful giveaway. Cherry-plums in summer often announce they are ripe by abruptly dropping off the tree to create a carpet of yellow on the ground. Being small fruit, they are fairly undamaged by this; they can even be harvested by laying a sheet under the tree and shaking it. Remember to clear away any fallen fruit you are not using.

Early pears and apples should be checked in summer for ripeness. Some, such as the apple Juneating, will start to ripen by the end of July. One sign is the first fruit falling (not the June drop), so a prerequisite may be to mow the grass so that you can spot them. (Remove the clippings, so as to avoid the fruit being covered in grass.) Notice if birds or wasps are hanging around nibbling at fruit, especially early pears – they are good at spotting the ones that are ready. These pears need to be picked and eaten soon, as they can quickly go brown inside. There is more in the next chapter about ripening and harvest.

## Other summer orchard tasks

Ideally, summer should find you looking out at trees with a good covering of healthy, dark green leaves (and paler green extension growth reaching for the light), plus a smattering of well-spaced fruit. If you can see something else, beware of the following:

- curled-up leaves, usually due to aphids, especially on cherries and plums; take appropriate action
- dead twigs, which could mean canker or scab
- broken branches, which may be due to failure to thin the fruit

Peaches are one of the first crops to harvest in early July.

An early ripener to watch for is the apple George Cave.

When wasps start nibbling, you know these russet pears are ripe.

- yellowing, or drooping, leaves, which may be caused by drought or root damage.

Now is the time to note and deal with any problems. Put out earwig lairs of corrugated card inside a plastic bottle hung upside down in the tree, for earwigs are good predators of aphids. Hanging jars of syrup in or near plum trees help to distract wasps from the fruit. You will find more help with pests and diseases in Chapters 10 and 11.

Watering may be needed in times of drought, even for well-established trees, but especially with newly planted ones. If there is not much rain, a bucket a week for all new trees is really important. Make sure that the weed-free circle you have created around these young trees does not get overgrown in summer. If it already has, don't dig too deeply when putting it right, as you may damage the surface roots of the tree. Weed with care! Mulch mats are a great help here, though do be wary of making a cosy home for voles.

Check the tightness of ties on young trees, loosening them if needed. Otherwise, growth will be restricted and tree health endangered. Identify – and label – your trees. After a couple of years, labels get lost or become unreadable and, if you're like us, your memory of exactly what tree is where becomes hazy.

You may have inherited some mystery trees and would like to know what they are. In summer, many orchard and gardening groups hold Apple Days, where an expert may be present to shed light on all your mysteries. So, before the event, pick some representative fruit, avoiding lop-sided ones that are the result of poor pollination. Make sure that you include the whole stalk (these can be a diagnostic) and some leaves, as well as noting the date of ripening, the age of the tree if known and where it is growing. One fruit isn't enough – these are not supermarket-style clones and your expert will need to see the range of variation. Size, base colour, flush colour, flesh colour, shape, stalk, eye, taste and smell are all used to pin a name on your apple.

Look out for aphids on your cherry leaves.

Can you still read the label?

If you can't find an Apple Day expert, or are looking to name other fruits, try the website www.fruitid.com.[7] It can look confusing as there are so many photos of fruits, but works well. There are thousands of varieties of apple alone, so there are no guarantees that you will get an answer. DNA analysis from leaves can be undertaken at a price, to match with DNA from the National Fruit Collection[8] in Kent. If your 'mystree' is not in the collection (maybe a seedling or a 'lost' variety), or the match is inconclusive, it will stay a 'mystree' – but may be even more valuable for that! Diversity is all …

## Scrump or share?

As a Devonshire man, Andrew is almost pathologically inclined to steal fruit – or 'scrump' it, as the term goes. He relates that he was born next to a cider orchard, but as a child he didn't appreciate that cider apples are not quite the same as eaters. An early scrumping experiment with the sours ended with severe tummy ache as a result – but it didn't put him off! One of our best-known Carse of Gowrie apples, the Bloody Ploughman, is so named because a ploughman, weary from his labours, took a shortcut home through the orchard of Megginch Castle. He picked an apple for refreshment, then another, then decided to fill his smock to take some home for the wife. Megginch was a big orchard (and is even bigger today) and the ploughman deemed that there were enough to share. Sadly, the gamekeeper was also taking a cut through the orchard and caught him red-handed. Out came the gun – bang! – and the Bloody Ploughman was born. Where the scrumped apples scattered, seedlings eventually grew up, bearing a new apple, dark red and deeply ribbed, with the flesh inside blood-streaked. Bloody Ploughman is a crisp, juicy apple and to this day it's better eaten straight from the tree – before you get caught!

So, from the West Country to northern Scotland, the ownership of fruit can be a grey area. If it hangs over a wall, does it belong to everyone? No one has

*(continued)*

The Bloody Ploughman, at home in Gas Brae Linear Orchard, Errol, Carse of Gowrie.

will put out baskets of surplus for neighbours or passers-by to help themselves, though some would rather see their fruit rot than share, sadly. In Central Europe, especially Czechia, the rural byways are planted deliberately with fruit trees and although some are 'owned' by a particular household, the ethos is that anyone needing refreshment can help themselves.

When we were young and eager horticulture students, people were just beginning to ask why local councils planted every kind of fancy and gastronomically useless ornamental cherry or similar as 'street trees', but never a tree that bore fruit that people could use. The reason given was 'If we did that, people would just eat the fruit.' Heaven help us! We're glad to say that some councils and even housing departments have begun to see the Kafkaesque illogic here and fruit trees are being planted near people's homes to share, not scrump. We've even heard of folk going out to 'guerrilla-graft' scions of edible cherries on to 'the cooncil's street trees', but couldn't possibly comment.

been prosecuted for scrumping in England since 1829. Nearly every fruit-tree owner knows what it's like to have more fruit than they can eat. Many

## Chapter Eight

# From Tree to Table

So, let's hope that all has gone well with your selection, planting, blossom time and summer management! At some stage, you will get to enjoy the produce of all those labours – but an orchard groaning with fruit can be a daunting prospect. When will you pick it – and how? What will you do with it then? How long will it keep?

## Is it ripe and ready to pick?

Confusingly, being ripe and ready to pick are not necessarily the same thing. If you were a commercial fruit grower producing for a supermarket chain, you would be at pains to make sure that the fruit was *not* ripe when picked. For the amateur, some varieties – especially late apples and most pears – are also best ripened off the tree. Many pears if left to ripen on the tree look fantastic on the outside, but cut them in half and the inside is brown and mushy. In Scotland, where it's a common phenomenon in the older Scottish varieties, we say the fruit has 'gone sleepy'. Very early pears, such as Jargonelle or Beth, ripen – and start to rot – so precipitously that you have to be on your guard and eat them immediately they are ready.

### The ripening process

A quick look at the processes involved in ripening will help to explain the problem. Fruit is a part of the growing plant and therefore the cells in the fruit are respiring – exchanging carbon dioxide and oxygen to release energy – all the time. The balance of carbon dioxide to oxygen alters as the fruit increases in size, until another gas – ethylene – is produced. Ethylene is a plant hormone and signals the start of the ripening process, called the climacteric.

Once ethylene production has started, it can't be stopped. The fruit will get ripe. Ethylene is also behind a process called abscission in autumn, that is, the fall of leaves and the separation of fruit from the branch. So, the commercial producer has a problem, in that they need to deliver fruit that has not started to 'go

With russet apples, look for the colour beneath the russeting.

These Perthshire pears were picked late and are showing signs of 'going sleepy'.

of record-keeping. We watch to see the first fruit fall. They are likely to be the damaged ones, so destined for the birds anyway, but they give an indicator that the bulk of the crop will soon be ready. Check the fruit still on the tree by gently lifting them upward, with your thumb against the stalk. If they are ready, they will detach easily, with a little fruit stalk. If you have to tug and wrench, with leaves and twigs coming away as well, you are too early. With pears, watch out for the first signs of 'give', or softness at the stalk end of the fruit. If the softness is obvious, it may be too late and the inside has already turned brown and 'sleepy'.

Don't be taken in by colour. Not all apples, for example, go rosy-red or flushed. Red colouring is more likely to be due to a spell of sunny weather and the fruit being on the south side of the tree, rather than them being ripe. A change in the background colour from green to a yellowish green is a more likely indicator of readiness.

over', or senesce. Delaying the production of ethylene during storage, by using growth-retardants, or, more commonly, by cooling the picked fruit rapidly in bulk containers and keeping it in a Controlled Atmosphere (CA) environment with temperatures between 30 and 40°F (−1–4°C), with strictly controlled levels of humidity, oxygen and carbon dioxide, the marketable life of a fruit crop is prolonged. There is a reason why shop-bought fruit may taste unripe. It is. Ripening only starts when the fruit is put on display.

## When shall I pick the crop?

With the proviso given above, that some varieties are best picked under-ripe, you need to be on constant watch. You could make yourself aware of the average timescale between first flowering and ripening, but if you have a lot of trees and not much time, that's a lot

Test the stalk end for softening on pears.

Apple Bloody Ploughman is dark red – but not ripe till the ploughman's blood has stained the flesh!

With stone fruit, a gentle squeeze can be a giveaway. We harvest all our peaches as soon as the flesh can be lightly depressed, as it's heart-rending to see a massive juicy peach splattered on the floor. If any don't ripen, they make delicious chutney. Plums and damsons that feel like bullets aren't ready. Sadly, the birds in our garden can time cherry-picking to the hour – they are all gone by the time we arrive!

## Picking by hand

If your aim is to store the fruit for any length of time, you need to take care of it. Bruised fruit will soon start to rot in storage and must be used right away. It helps to have a fruit apron with a large front pocket, or fruit-picking bags with shoulder straps or harnesses, which leave the hands free to hold on to the fruit. Place the picked fruit gently – chucking apples into a box as if they were potatoes will not work and don't be fooled by pictures of cider apples

being bulk-loaded in a happy-go-lucky manner, as these are not intended for storage.

Fruit that's out of reach presents a bigger problem and inevitably while pulling off one ripe fruit, two or three others will become detached and crash to the ground. We favour having as much of the crop within reach from ground level as possible, which is down to choosing the right rootstock and performing the correct training and pruning. It's also a reason to thin overcrowded fruit clusters early in the summer. The remaining fruit will be larger, easier to handle and less likely to be accidentally dislodged and shower down on you. However, there will be scenarios where you will need extendable fruit-picking poles for getting to at least some of the high-up fruit, or ladders. If using ladders, get proper orchard ladders for stability and do your risk assessment, especially if working with community groups.

If that sounds a bit of a worry, remember that apples for cider, or pears for perry, do not have to be in pristine condition. Giving the tree a good shake may be all that is needed in order to harvest a crop.

Our home-made harvesting tool for fruit on tall trees.

## Machine-picking

Sticking with cider for a moment, that's exactly what commercial orchardists do with their harvesting machines – give the trees a good shake. Mechanical tree shakers are self-contained tractor-mounted units, with two operators. One drives the tractor, the other wraps a specialised cloth sling, which does not carry a risk of damage to bark, round the trunk of each tree. For cider makers, whose requirements for fruit quality differ from fruit sellers, it is usual for the fruit then to be collected from the ground. Where fruit must not be bruised or damaged, there will be a conveyor-type pick-up system to get rid of excess stems and foliage and move the fruit gently from tree to box.

## Storing fruit

Assuming that you don't have the automated rapid cooling apparatus and controlled atmosphere units of the commercial grower, the first thing you need to work out is which varieties of apple and pear are worth storing for any length of time. Soft fruit such as damsons or plums won't store. They ripen quickly and have to be used or processed quickly as well. Apples vary, and your personal experience and that of others will eventually tell you what can be safely stored for a few months or even longer. There are a few clues:

- early varieties tend not to be keepers
- apples with thin, easily-bruised skins do not keep well
- late varieties are mostly suitable for storage
- russet apples, being both late and with thick, leathery, russety skins, usually improve with storing

Note that apples stored for a long time may look wizened and unappetising, but usually remain exquisite when peeled!

Much the same is true of pears – the softer and juicier they are, the better advised you are to eat them immediately, or preserve them in some way. Remember always the hard pear's habit of looking good on the outside, but being 'sleepy' inside; avoid storing varieties, such as Craig's Favourite or Goud Knap, that are prone to this. Good storing pears are thin on the ground, compared to apples.

## Where to store and how

Temperature is important. Apples and pears keep for longer if they are in a cool place, but they must not be somewhere likely to freeze – temperatures of more than 1–2°C below freezing will cause damage and the breakdown of tissues. Many of us find a frost-free shed, outhouse or unheated greenhouse suitable, while others make use of an unheated room in the

When the harvest starts, you need to get trays and bags organised.

Open storage allows you to check for rotting fruit easily.

**Table 4: A selection of varieties showing picking time and storage period**

| Variety | Picking time | Store for |
|---|---|---|
| Apple Arbroath (Oslin) | Late August/early September | No more than a month |
| Apple Arthur Turner | September | A month to six weeks |
| Apple Beauty of Bath | Late August | A day if you're lucky … |
| Apple Bloody Ploughman | September | A month or two – goes wrinkly but still tastes good |
| Apple Bramley's Seedling | October | Almost forever … well into late spring in the cool, or longer |
| Apple Cox's Orange Pippin | October | At least till Christmas – longer in cool place |
| Apple Egremont Russet | Early October | Up to Christmas – may need peeling after |
| Apple Fiesta | Early October | Several months in a cool place |
| Apple Grenadier | Late August | Not much more than a month |
| Apple Hawthorndon | Mid/late September | Up to Christmas |
| Apple James Grieve | Mid-September | Till New Year, just |
| Apple Laxton's Fortune | September | Maybe to mid-December |
| Apple Reinette Grise de la Creuse | Late October/early November | Right until May, getting sweeter as time passes |
| Apple Ribston Pippin | October | Up to three months |
| Apple Sunset | September/October | Till January |
| Apple Worcester Pearmain | Mid/late September | Good for at least a month, but can be kept till New Year or beyond in cool |
| Pear Concorde | Late September/October | Till mid-November |
| Pear Conference | Late September/early October | Maybe a month in cool |
| Pear Jargonelle | August | Not suitable for storing |
| Pear Williams Bon Chretien | September | Eat straight from tree |
| Pear Winter Nelis | October/early November | Two to three months in cool |

house. Sadly, our changing climate is making it a challenge to find stores with even, cool temperatures. Be alert for unexpected temperature rises in winter and keep checking the fruit for any becoming overripe.

The storing room has to be vermin- and bird-proof, for obvious reasons. We like to use our summer house, but if someone leaves the door ajar by mistake, a tray of apples is soon got at by our over-tame blackbirds. Keep a watch for mice, which can readily manoeuvre themselves through the eye of a darning needle if there's an apple on the other side of it. Do not even dream of storing windfalls, scabby, blemished or bruised fruit. They will rot quickly and spread the problem to all the sound fruit. Use them up in juice or jelly. Only 100 per cent sound and healthy fruit should go into store.

Should the fruit be allowed to touch each other? A debatable point. Many gardeners are proud to

Beauty of Bath apples are a colourful early eater, but don't try to store them.

Apple storage shelves for saving space.

wrap each fruit individually and maintain social distancing between them in storage. Undoubtedly, this will help, but if every apple you store is guaranteed sound and undamaged, it may not be necessary. We have known plenty of people who store their keepers in plastic carrier bags and get away with it – probably because they take care with what goes in the bags and have ideal storage conditions to boot. Remember, if all your fruit are wrapped, you have to unwrap each one to check it; though, likewise, who knows what's festering away at the bottom of a carrier bag?

What do we do? We use open trays. The fruit are touching, but each one is visible … and we *check regularly*. Despite our best efforts only to store the most suitable fruit, micro-organisms creep in unnoticed. When we spot an apple starting to deteriorate, it has one of three destinations: the good bits salvaged for crumble or cake; the bird table or lawn for the blackbirds and fieldfares; or the compost heap. Accept that you won't win them all and that these final destinations are not the same as food waste.

Do not store damaged or blemished fruit.

Rats and mice can cause considerable damage to stored fruit.

## Options for the non-keepers

There is a surprisingly large range of options for preserving orchard gluts:

- freezing
- bottling
- drying
- chutneys and pickles
- jams and jellies
- juicing
- fermenting

We will deal will them in turn.

### Freezing fruit

Almost all fruit can be cooked and stored in the freezer, ready for use in pies, crumbles and the like throughout winter, spring and summer, until the next year's crop arrives. We make a point of finishing up one year's harvest before starting to lay down the next, but do know people who have several years' worth squirrelled away. It's possible to fill a number of freezers very quickly in a good year, so it's best not to have freezing as the only method of preservation. You may not want to stew some fruit; peaches, plums and other stone fruit can be halved or sliced, stone removed, then frozen in a light sugar syrup. Don't make this too concentrated with sugar, as syrup needs very low temperatures to freeze. If using this method, slightly under-ripe fruit works best and use within six months.

Freezing fruit raw and unprocessed is something to consider as a quick way to deal with a glut. We do it with soft fruit, but some people freeze whole apples for juicing or cider-making later. A frozen whole apple won't come out as a crisp eater, of course.

### Bottling

Bottling is a sound and traditional method of preserving food, which requires no freezer space. We have successfully bottled plums, peaches, damsons and small pears. There are various methods, but our favourite goes like this:

1. Sterilise the jars (we use a brewer's sterilant, which is quick and effective, but whatever works for you is fine).
2. Use only clean, under-ripe fruit, prepared. Plums are halved and stoned. Peaches are sliced and skinned. Pears are quartered, cored and peeled.
3. Pack the jars tightly with fruit.
4. Make up a syrup (250g to 600ml [8.8oz to 1pt] water for plums, pears or sliced apples; 125g to 600ml [4.4oz to 1pt] for peaches and apricots), making sure that there is plenty spare. Cover the fruit in jars with syrup.
5. Place in a cool oven at 150°C (300°F) for forty to sixty minutes, lids loose but not sealed down.
6. Remove jars one at a time and top up with more boiling syrup or water where the fruit has shrunk.
7. Clip or screw down jars and do not touch or move them for a day. A vacuum seal should form as the contents cool.
8. After this time, check that the lids are sealed and don't come away from the jar. If all is well, stash the jars in a cupboard for resurrection as Christmas trifle ingredients fresh from the orchard!

We use Kilner-type jars with rubber rings and clips, or the screw-down kinds. Be warned, the rubber rings are difficult to break the seal on and will need to be regularly replaced.

Preserving jars come in many shapes and sizes.

Dried apple rings capture the colours and intensify the sweetness of fresh fruit.

## Drying

This can take a bit of time, but is really worth doing. A proportion of our apples are always turned into dried apple rings. Peel, core and slice thinly, one apple at a time. Immediately dip the slices into a mild salt solution, which not only prevents them discolouring too much, it also kills off any moulds that might reduce the longevity of the apple rings. Then set them to dry. We use a dehydrator, but the bottom of a range is said to be good, as is hanging them above a wood-burner. Even festering on the top of school radiators does the job eventually! Apple rings will not go crispy – if they do, you've burnt them – but when they are leathery and completely dry to the touch they can be packed into jars and shelved. We have never known them last less than a year and they are fantastic in porridge, or on long winter walks.

If you have a mixture of fruits, pulp them and spread a thin layer over greaseproof paper in a baking tray, in order to make fruit leather. I've found that the dehydrator takes too long, so usually put the tray in the oven while it's cooling down, but different fruit combinations have different requirements. Pear pulp is particularly good in fruit-leather making. When it's dry – leathery of course – peel it away from the greaseproof, rolling it up as you go, then slice it for high-energy snacks.

One drying technique we haven't tried (due to memories of school dinners and a preference for damsons and plums raw) is drying these stone fruit to make prunes. But who knows? Perhaps in a few years, it might be that drying fruit on the roof, as seen in Mediterranean climates, will become a thing in Britain, too.

## Chutneys and pickles

Adding fruit to chutneys works well and is a good way to use all those bits of fruit left after the damaged or scabby parts have been cut off. Peach chutney is one of our annual favourite sweet chutneys. Chopped pears, dessert apples, plums and cherries are all great ingredients for inventing a whole range of mixed chutneys. If you use cooking apples, the 'froth' makes a wonderful thick base for piccalilli. You can make a fruit sauce with apples and pears cooked and sieved with tomatoes and onions, while plum sauce is a wonderfully decadent accompaniment to Sunday dinner.

Walnuts for pickling are taken from the tree in summer, way before the shells have started to harden, and the whole immature fruit is used. After several days in brine, followed by storage in spiced vinegar, they are delectable! In theory, almost anything can be pickled, but pickled plums are famed in Japanese cuisine, while pickled cherries or grapes give a startling contrast of sweet and acid flavours. You might want to avoid or go light on ingredients for subtle-tasting fruit like apricots. Aim to use up fruit pickles before they get to the stage of being soggy bits tasting only of vinegar.

## Jams, jellies and preserves

We don't want to state the obvious, but most jams are based on fruit, so a liking for jam definitely helps when processing the orchard harvest. Before ingredients were listed and regulated by law, Clyde Valley Strawberry Jam was made using a significant amount of apple pulp. This helped set the jam and the strawberries were often grown in rows between the orchard trees.

There are many jam recipes to choose from. Jellies are even easier and apple jelly is our last resort to use up all the remaining apples that won't store. Just cut up the washed apples into chunks, cover with water and cook till soft. As a guide, 1ltr (1.8pt) to 1kg (2.2lb) of apples works well. Any apple variety can be used, but be sure to include a few cookers to provide the pectin needed to set the jelly. Then strain the liquid through muslin or a jelly bag overnight into a measuring jug. Add about 500g (17oz) of sugar to every 600ml (1pt) of strained juice and boil till setting point is reached. We tend to divide up the liquid

Fruit chutneys are colourful and delicious.

A variety of apple jellies.

# Fruit preserves

Following is a selection of our favourite fruit preserves.

### Peach chutney

We use the undamaged sides of the peaches that have dropped to the floor and also the small, still-hard ones that are the last on the tree and not really worthy of whipped cream. The softer fruit help to make a thick, succulent matrix for the chutney, but the hard ones keep their shape and give it some bite. The quantities are vague, because it depends how many peaches you have to spare and, anyway, we make it up as we go along.

Soak a handful or two of raisins or sultanas for twenty-four hours before you start. Chop a red onion (or two) into smallish pieces and cut the peaches into chunks. Put into a large pan with the raisins, then toss the lot in ground turmeric, coriander and cumin powder. Be subtle with the spices, because you don't want to drown the fruit flavour. A good curry powder can be used instead. Add two to three tablespoons of light brown sugar, a cup of cider vinegar, half a cup of water and salt to taste, then start to heat and cook the chutney. We leave the salt until later, because it's all a bit experimental and you can get it just right once the fruit is cooked. The salt and vinegar are the key preservatives, however, so don't leave either out.

It may take a while, but the chutney isn't ready until it's so thick that you can draw the spoon across the base of the pan and leave a bare trail. Don't rush it, or turn the heat up too high – nothing worse than a burnt taste in your chutney. When done, leave to cool slightly, before pouring into hot, sterilised glass jars. If they have metal lids, place a piece of greaseproof paper between the glass and the lid, as the acid vinegar can corrode the lid.

Our method may sound a bit hit and miss, but we've never had a failure.

### Savoury fruit sauce

This can be made with plums or damsons and it's delectable. It is also a nice quick way to use up some of the overburden of apples – dessert apples are best, but pears can be used as well.

Stone and skin the plums by part-boiling and sliding the flesh away from the skins (you don't have to get every bit). If using apples or pears, peel and chop roughly.

Gently fry some finely chopped shallots or a sweet red onion, adding two cloves of chopped or minced garlic. Add half a teaspoon of ground cinnamon, a few cloves (to be taken out later) and half a teaspoon of ground cardamom if you have it. Stir, then add four or five skinned chopped tomatoes. Bubble that lot along for at least five minutes, then add the fruit (aim for at least double the volume of fruit to tomatoes). Cook together for another ten minutes until the sauce is the consistency you want, then season with salt and pepper to taste. Serve hot or cold as an accompaniment to any main course.

### Sweet chilli apple jelly

Add 500g (17oz) of white sugar to 600ml (1pt) of strained apple juice. If you are using fresh chilli, use a red one and slice it in half, removing the stalk and most of the seeds (more chillis can be used according to your tolerance to heat). Blanch the chilli by pouring boiling water over it for a few moments – this helps to stop any moulds on the skin transferring to the sugary jelly. Pop the chilli into the sugar/juice mixture and bring it to the boil in a large pan. Turn down and simmer till setting point is reached. Remove the chilli and pour the jelly into hot, sterilised jars. You can add thin slices or flakes of another blanched red chilli to the jar for decoration.

If you're using dried chillis, remember that though they are small, they are hotter than fresh ones. Do not measure the chilli out by volume! Note that chilli powder won't work.

and add herbs (either chopped or in a muslin bag to take out later) to make different flavoured jellies. Our favourites are mint, chilli and rosemary, but we haven't tried them all yet!

## Juicing

If you have a sizeable orchard, or combine in a cooperative with other orchards or local enthusiasts, juicing is a great option for apples or pears. A community juicing day is great fun and a real eye-opener for people who think that apple juice comes in a supermarket carton – they are invariably converted to the real thing, even if that real thing is a sludgy brown and has bits in it!

There are two stages to preparing excellent apple juice – crushing the apples and pressing the juice out – and one ingredient. Apples. The fruit can be crushed using an electric scratter (a good investment when lots of fruit is involved), a hand-turned crusher, a mincer, a wooden post, or a 10kg (22lb) weight. You will also need a cider press. The juice will run freely into a bucket and the fun begins, for there will be far too much to drink all in one go.

If you don't want to turn the juice into alcohol, you will probably want it to look a bit better than the mud-coloured liquid in the bucket. You could:

A community apple-pressing event.

Mashing and pressing apples can be fun for families.

- Allow the solids to settle and decant or siphon off the clear liquid. With some apples this will happen overnight, but others take days to clear, during which time the juice could start to ferment.
- Strain it through a jelly bag or muslin but *don't squeeze*. The cloudy sediment will be pushed through too if you do that.
- Add pectolase, an enzyme that destroys pectin. Pectin, as well as making jams set, causes much of the haziness in juice. Siphon off the clear liquid after twenty-four hours.

If you just bottle the juice now and stick it in a cupboard, it will ferment, not always becoming something you would want to drink. We use well-cleaned cardboard milk cartons, leave a space for expansion and put them in one of the freezers. When you get them out in winter, it is like drinking a glass of sunshine.

Bottling juice is time-consuming, but rewarding.

Apple juice will store longer if pasteurised.

But the proper route – essential if you have plans to sell your juice – is to pasteurise it. On a small scale, use clean, sterilised glass bottles, pour in the juice and stand them in a water bath. Add cold water to the water bath and heat to 70°C (158°F). Hold that temperature for twenty minutes. Never heat the juice directly. If you are producing a saleable product, you might want to add lemon juice from the start, so that the juice is not so brown. It is tannin in the fruit that causes the browning and is completely natural. Some varieties contain more tannin than others, so might be deselected for juicing on that basis. Citric acid can also be added as an extra preservative.

## Fermentation and alcoholic beverages

If your apple juice ferments, it will become cider. The quality, sweetness, strength and palatability of said cider, though, will depend on a number of things,

Home-made pasteuriser does the job.

the most important of which is what apples went into the juicer. Professional cider-makers will use a mixture of sweet, bitter and sour apple varieties to get the finished product just right, with a fine balance between 'sharps', 'bitter-sharps' – which have a high tannin content and lend an astringent taste – and 'sweets' or 'bittersweets', also high in tannin but giving cider a mellow, full-bodied flavour. Cider apples – rarely used for any other purpose – have a long history of breeding and include some very old and romantic-sounding varieties (see Table 5).

However, cider trees can be difficult to get hold of and, on a domestic scale, you can make a very acceptable cider by just using a mixture of whatever apples you happen to have. We would recommend, though, that some sharp cookers such as Bramley, or even astringent crab apples, are always part of the mix, as cider based purely on dessert apples will be sweet, but insipid. Often 'wildings' sprouting out of a hedgerow have this useful astringency, even though they may not be great to eat. There are, we know, some commercial ciders based on a single variety of apple. We don't know how they do it, but feel free to experiment! Whatever apples you use, they need to be fully ripe. Even overripe and slightly bruised apples can go into cider, but they must be sound and not rotten.

Your next choice in the cider-making process will be whether to allow the wild yeasts living on the skin of the fruit to do the fermenting. If you fill a one-gallon demijohn right to the top with apple juice, plug the top with cotton wool and leave it, it will start fermenting in a few days. But sometimes it stops the day after – fermentation has 'stuck', or maybe there aren't enough yeasts to complete the job. A worse possibility is that among the wild yeasts there are some microbes that, undetected, will make the cider taste pretty revolting, whether fermentation completes or not. The alternative is to sterilise the juice using sulphur dioxide (in the form of powdered sodium metabisulphite or Campden tablets), leave it for a few days, then add dried yeast (cider yeast, champagne yeast, wine yeast, or, only if you have

## Table 5: A cider-maker's dozen

Following is our selection of traditional and not so traditional varieties of apples to experiment with when making cider. Note that the list is not exhaustive!

| | |
|---|---|
| **Brown's Apple** | A sharp, aromatic, Devon cider apple; has some resistance to scab |
| **Camelot** | A mild bittersweet from Somerset, also a good cooker |
| **Dabinett** | Widely planted aromatic bittersweet from Somerset |
| **Foxwhelp** | Old traditional bitter-sharp cider apple from Gloucestershire and Herefordshire |
| **Katy** | Popular sweet and juicy apple from Sweden, much used in sweet single-variety ciders |
| **Keswick Codlin** | Early fruiting, reliable apple producing lots of juice; from north-west England |
| **Kingston Black** | A West Country bitter-sharp, producing very dark, small apples |
| **Lord Derby** | Crisp and juicy English cooking apple, widely grown and reliable |
| **Slack-ma-Girdle** | A Devon sweet cider apple. Who wouldn't want a cider apple with a name like this? |
| **Thomas Jeffrey** | Pretty dessert apple, copiously juicy but best saved for cider; from Scotland |
| **Tom Putt** | A dual-purpose apple used for cooking, eating and cider, originating in the West Country |
| **Yarlington Mill** | A reliable Somerset cider apple; a late bittersweet |

no other, brewer's yeast). Fermentation should start vigorously and continue for a week or two. When it has calmed down and brown froth has stopped oozing over the table, exchange the cotton wool plugs for a civilised airlock. We have made some very good cider using both natural fermentation and the sterilisation method, but we have also made some terrible stuff.

After a couple of weeks, the solids will start to settle and the fermenting juice begins to clear. Then it's time to rack, or siphon, the clear cider from the solids into another demijohn. Once fermentation has stopped, you can rack it into sterilised bottles. Here you have another choice. By adding half a tea-spoon of sugar to each bottle, you will encourage a little secondary fermentation and get sparkling cider. The easiest way to add the sugar is to calculate how much you need for the entire demijohn and dissolve it into some of the cider, adding the syrup back in before bottling. Make sure that you have

Cider jars gently bubbling with juice.

Perry pears are distinct and not good for eating.

proper, pressure-proof, swing-top bottles, or repurpose plastic fizzy drinks bottles if you do this – you don't want glass bottles exploding. If you like still cider, forget the sugar priming. You can drink the cider after a few weeks, although some do improve with keeping.

This is, of course, a very basic outline of how to make cider. You may want to go into much more detail, create vintage ciders, subtle blends or curiously flavoured ones, or start a commercial enterprise. We would strongly suggest that you read more deeply – *Real Cidermaking on a Small Scale* by Michael Pooley and John Lomax[9] is a good place to start. We would also advise doing a practical cider-making course.

Making perry – the pear equivalent to cider – follows roughly the same procedures, but can turn out to be rather insipid unless proper, fabulously named, perry pears are used. Our usual dessert pears, if used, would require tannin and acid to be added to make a worthwhile drink. Michael Pooley discourages using a mix of pears, too – unlike apples, they really don't blend at all well.

Beyond the scope of this book, but well worth remembering, is the potential of orchard fruit to flavour spirits and create comforting winter warmers,

These windfall plums could make a good slivovitz.

such as damson gin, plum brandy (slivovitz), peach vodka, and apricot or cherry brandy.

So, there is no shortage of things to do with a glut of fruit from your orchard!

## Cider and perry traditions

Cider is fermented apple juice. That's it. The term 'apple cider' is a tautology and the fashion for very sweet cider flavoured and made even sweeter by the addition of various other fruits and concentrates is okay if you like that sort of thing, but don't mistake it for the real thing. Apple wine is not cider, either. Cider – or at any rate home-made and craft cider – does not have added water or sugar. Likewise, there is no such thing as 'pear cider'. You can have cider with added pear flavouring, or you can have fermented pear juice, which is called perry, and there's an end to that.

Cider in a recognisable form has been around since the thirteenth century at least and probably far longer, but using crab apples. It would not have taken much to develop the making of it, as apples will turn themselves into cider very readily! We no longer have to fret about the safety of our drinking water in these islands, so drinking cider is a luxury, not a necessity, and perhaps our tastes have become more sophisticated. 'Rough' or 'scrumpy' cider, if it's the real deal, does not appeal to everyone's palate, but cider varies in sweetness, flavour and sparkle enormously, depending on what apples are in it, how long the fermentation lasted and whether a secondary fermentation was started in the bottle to make it sparkling. Even slight climatic differences among ciders from dry East Anglia and the traditional ciders of the wetter regions of Herefordshire, Ireland or the West Country account for cider diversity. There is a cider for all tastes.

One of the first and best cider apples was the Redstreak, of which there are several variants. Like many cider apples, Redstreaks are not the result of deliberate breeding, but 'wildings' – chance offspring of a thrown-away apple core. Cider orchards traditionally contain tall, magnificent trees, such as Foxwhelp and Yarlington Mill, and so do perry pear orchards, with trees like Huffcap, Thorn and Green Horse. Apples and pears were traditionally crushed in a hand- or horse-powered wooden press and the juice fermented in wooden barrels.

Is there any truth in the tales of adding a dead rat or two to the barrel? Possibly! Fermentation sometimes 'sticks', when nutrient levels run out for the yeast. Traditional cider-makers were wont to hang a leg of mutton in the barrel, to break down in the acid juice slowly. Soluble amino nitrogen from the meat provided the yeasts, which are fungal organisms, with the 'oomph' to keep fermenting the cider to dryness. Nowadays, you can buy yeast nutrient ... but we wonder what's in it!

The best-known cider tradition is wassailing ... more of that in Chapter 11.

## Chapter Nine

# Winter Pruning and Taming Tangled Trees

## The fruit tree in winter

Although the orchard owner has been focused on the crop of fruit through late summer and autumn, the fruit trees themselves have a different focus. They are planning for next year's crop – and, once again, it is buds that are at the centre of things. Remember, healthy buds are the key to next year's flowering and fruiting. They are formed in July and August in the gap between leaf stalks and the main stem. Keeping the trees healthy at that time by a foliar feed will benefit next year's growth. Autumn sunlight matures the buds and the first few frosts ready them for winter. It is time for the buds to rest, for growth to cease and the leaves to fall. The terminal bud on each branch should have fully formed. The tree enters the period known as dormancy.

The dormant period is the correct time to prune all free-standing pip fruit such as apples and pears. It's not the right time to prune stone fruit such as plums and cherries, as we have seen, because of the risk of introducing bacterial canker and fungal diseases such as silverleaf. But for all fruit trees, it is very good practice to ensure that fallen leaves and fruit are swept up and taken away to compost in closed bins before winter comes. This is because spores of many fungal diseases overwinter happily on leaves and windfalls, just waiting to reinfect the trees in spring. It's also quite common to slip and slide all over the place on fallen apples and there are enough hazards in winter pruning – so tidy the area first!

## Regular winter pruning

The following items are needed for successful winter pruning:

- a good pruning saw with a safety holster – for getting in-between branches easily; bow saws are usually too big
- good-quality, sharp, clean secateurs
- loppers – long armed – for larger branches, although a cut made by a pruning saw will often be cleaner and better controlled
- long or extendable loppers or pruning saws for working on the higher branches
- a purpose-made three-legged orchard ladder for taller trees
- a clean rag and methylated spirits or alcohol to wipe tools as you go from tree to tree – this prevents spreading disease
- a first-aid kit and gloves

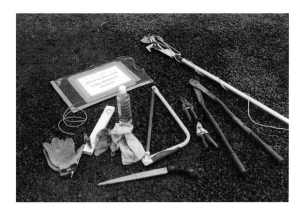

Pruning tools.

For young trees that have not been neglected, there may be little to do, especially if summer pruning has taken place, but the following method explains regular winter pruning:

- Walk around the tree. Observe the strong shoots, the weak ones, the ones heading off in an inconvenient direction. Think. You will soon learn to 'get your eye in' and see what needs doing. *Never* dive in snip-snipping with a pair of secateurs – you are most likely to snip away your next year's crop, incite growth the following year where you don't want it and thwart your own intentions.
- Identify the aim of the gardener who first trained the tree. With luck, it'll be you and you will remember, but if you've inherited your orchard, decide whether a tree's formative pruning was to produce an open centre, a low standard or a central leader. Your aim will usually be to prune to keep this form.
- Remove diseased branches and shoots, particularly if showing symptoms of canker or scab (*see* Chapter 11). Take off any fruit that have rotted but still hang on the tree. Dispose of this diseased material away from the orchard – do not leave it lying around.
- Are the branches that make the main framework in good condition and well-spaced around the trunk? If there are too many on a young tree, take one out. On older trees, these will be a permanent framework. If you need to replace a framework branch, you could sometimes cut the existing one back to a strong bud going in the same direction. It's a good principle to renew a proportion of the framework branches in this way every year. If that option isn't available – maybe because the branch itself is damaged or diseased – you could select a new, long shoot that is growing vertically and tie it down to become a new branch in the framework. This is the technique described in Chapter 7.

- Start by taking out the heaviest unwanted branches in the middle. Drag them down through the tree and remove. This will help you to see what is going on and allow light into the tree.
- Look for branches that are shaded by the ones above. Take out larger branches, especially heavy ones in the top of the tree that shade everything. This may mean cutting them right back to where they arise and can feel a bit drastic. It isn't. It is not only a better solution than hesitant snipping at the branch, which doesn't remove the problem, it also saves you a lot of time. Remove all entirely shaded branches that are low on the tree, and any seriously drooping branches. The latter can be cut back to a more upright shoot if they are well-positioned.
- Thin out 'busy' areas, where too many crossing branches are creating shade and poor air circulation, especially in the centre of the tree and on the ends of long branches. This is a common

Heavy pruning leads to lots of growth the following year.

Canker on a main trunk is a serious problem.

situation in open-centre trained trees that have been a bit neglected – the tree seems hell-bent on filling up that hole in the middle! Again, use saws and loppers to remove whole errant branches before going for the detailed trimming, as you find it's not then needed.

- Vertical shoots will not give you much fruit. Unless trained by tying down, they will just keep growing upward. These water shoots often arise from previous pruning cuts and can crowd the centre of the tree, or the ends of lopped branches. Remove them, unless they are useful framework replacements. Shorter verticals can be tied down to become fruiting dards in the future if required – don't cut these back.
- Review your progress at intervals. Are there branches showing long bare stretches of wood? If so, consider removing the branch, or cutting it back to a shoot again. Balance the lengths of the remaining branches by walking around the tree and observing which ones are too far out of balance and cutting back accordingly, usually to a bud.
- Now work to leave the all-important short and medium-sized sublaterals that have a big fruit bud on the end. These are the dards and brindilles that are the main source of fruit next year. There may be too many for the health of the tree, so cutting back a third of them to a stub (which will regrow into a fruiting spur) each year renews them and keeps them free from disease.

Look to lighten the weight of branches on mature trees.

Pruning in the centre can lead to excess regrowth elsewhere.

Top-pruning a vigorous tree can lead to a burst of water shoots.

## Tip

Gauge how many fruiting buds there are on the tree before you start pruning. Too many? Prune some away or thin them out. Too few? Prune, or tuck under in spindle bushes, to encourage more fruiting buds to form. Don't prune out the fruiting dards on spindle bushes!

Short upright shoots can be tucked under to encourage fruiting.

Now, how is the tree looking? If your tree looks very neat and tidy, be worried! You have probably given it a haircut rather than pruned it, thus removing most of its fruiting wood. Don't succumb to the temptation to tip-prune or snip all the new shoots of a round-headed or open-centred tree in order to 'keep it under control'. For a start, it won't work; if you want keep the size of a tree in check, move to encouraging more horizontal branches. Second, this is orchard pruning, not topiary. A tree that has a sufficient amount of fruiting wood left after pruning will also fruit well and regularly – and should not be growing very much anyway. Snip away all the fruiting wood and the tree responds by growing bigger to get away from its 'hairdresser'!

## Pruning central leader trees on dwarf rootstocks

To keep this form at its productive best, we recommend that you:

- Carry out renewal pruning every year.
- Remove any suckers arising from the base of the tree.
- Remove low branches drooping too near the ground.
- Cut out diseased shoots.
- Cut or tie down very upright shoots.
- Cut thicker than thumb-sized, heavy, branches to a stub.
- Remove vigorous branches in the top of the tree.
- Annually, renew the leading shoot.
- Maintain the tree's 'A' shape by heading back or removing long shoots in the top of the tree that are starting to creep into alleys, or the space allocated to the next tree.
- With the remaining shoots, leave one-third, cut one-third back to a stub and cut one-third back to fruit buds.

*See also* Chapter 5 on training spindle-bush trees.

Tree suckers should be removed.

## Restorative pruning

It is worth noting that fruit trees, especially those planted on vigorous rootstocks, may live a long time. Plums rarely last longer than sixty years, but even that's much longer than popularly believed. Apples commonly keep going for 50–100 years, while pear trees can live and produce well for 200–300 years or longer, even if they are hollow. If you inherit one like that – or take on a neglected orchard with many old trees – cutting it down may be the easiest option, but not necessarily the best. Old trees may be the last remnants of historical varieties and can have significant landscape value, towering over a valley in a sea of blossom in spring. There is also the exponential increase in value to wildlife and local ecology that occurs as trees age.

Restoring an older tree can be a very rewarding project, although it does require a bit more skill, not

Spindle bush laden with fruit, but the lower branches are now too low.

Tie down branches to a nail on the post to make them more horizontal.

to mention equipment. And the tree may not be as terminally ill as its appearance suggests. It is perfectly normal for some trees like pears and plums to hollow out and survive or even thrive, while those that have blown down may continue to crop for many years so long as some of the roots remain in the ground. Whether to remove or to restore may hinge on the condition of the tree. If there is lots of vigorous growth, no matter how untidy, the tree is in good condition. But a tree showing very little growth may be a challenge to bring back.

## What are the problems?

You may encounter some of the following problems when trying to restore old trees:

Old plum tree at Priorwood Garden, Melrose.

You will need long-armed pruners to tackle neglected trees.

- Trees grown on vigorous rootstocks can be 25m (82ft) tall, or more.
- There will be far too much wood in the top of a neglected tree, making the crown too heavy even when not in fruit. This can lead to structural collapse, especially if the tree has started to become hollow. The weight and density of the crown also makes old trees more prone to windthrow.
- Long branches may be too heavy at the ends, especially when in fruit, and will be liable to break
- Overcrowded centres and tangled, shading branches will have reduced all light coming down the centre of the tree, affecting disease resistance, blossom and fruit formation.

It may sound contradictory, but you should actually make as few pruning cuts as possible. Every time you cut, a vigorous tree will respond the following year by throwing out even more shoots, which will grow fast, undo your good work and cause problems for years to come. Fruit trees do *not* respond well to pollarding – that is, cutting everything off at head height. The swarm of new shoots will not bear fruit and will be very difficult to deal with in succeeding years. But there may be one, or perhaps two, big branches that could be taken out completely to the trunk, whose removal lets loads of light back into the tree, reduces the weight of the crown and cuts out much of the tangle that is making the tree prone to fungal diseases. Walk around the tree and look for where one or two cuts could make all the difference.

Then walk around again. You are looking to thin and lighten the crown, not reduce height. With tall trees, keep a good awareness of safety. Long-armed pruners may help you to work from the ground, but are no easy option, requiring strength, lots of looking up and care. Don't let the sawn branches fall and rip through the canopy you are trying to preserve to crack you on the head, and when one of them gets tangled up in high branches, getting it down to ground level is no mean feat. To do the job properly – and even more importantly, safely – some climbing or ladder

work may be required. Proper orchard ladders with three leg supports can be very stable and have the advantage of being readily placed close to the trunk, where most of the cutting work will take place. Once thinning is complete and the crown is lightened, your aim is to reshape the tree to a balanced form.

Very old trees with hollow trunks often seem to develop a notable 'lean'. In exposed sites, they will be prone to windthrow and may need their tops cut back to save them from falling at the next storm. Due to the consequential shoots they will put up next year to compensate, if they are vigorous and healthy, their restoration will take several years as these shoots are steadily removed.

You may have a tree that's already succumbed to wind and gravity and is lying prostrate, but is still alive – maybe even thriving! We've often seen these propped up with forked sticks in a well-meaning attempt to fix the problem, but unless it's a younger tree and the fall has only just happened, you could easily do more harm than good. If the tree is not prostrate but has a decided lean, shorten the horizontal branches on the leaning side to reduce the weight of the crown and relieve pressure on the roots. Thin the

Open up the centre of congested trees.

This tree needs steady reduction of the taller shoots each year.

Even neglected and forgotten orchards can be coaxed back into production.

This mature tree needs to be pruned over a number of years.

After pruning, the tree could develop a more open and balanced form.

new upright shoots the tree will have produced; this will lighten the original head of the tree. Some of these new vertical shoots can be redeployed to form a new, roundish head for the leaning or prostrate tree. In forestry, such trees are known as 'phoenix' trees – you can't keep a good tree down! Take care not to let the vertical shoots predominate.

## A reminder about plums

The plum family should not be winter-pruned. Plums do not grow tidily, producing many long, thin, gangling branches that are not structurally strong, but as the trees are covered in dense foliage at the correct summer pruning time, these may not be spotted.

Then there's the issue that, even when you do notice a weak branch, it is covered in little embryonic plums that you don't want to lose. (This is one reason why plums rarely get pruned correctly, if at all.)

But those little plumlets as they grow put such weight on a thin branch that it partly snaps, making 'elbows' from the branch breakage. These broken branches, which you may now be seeing for the first time, are already putting the tree at risk of disease attack, so it may be best to tidy them up whenever spotted, even in winter, before they split from the trunk and make the wound larger. Waiting till the sap is rising in early spring may be a good option, if you safely can. This is a good reason to remember to prune plums in the summer, even if a few plum puddings are sacrificed!

If plums are not thinned or pruned in summer, branches may break.

## Apples at Hallowe'en

The connection between apples and Hallowe'en is both obvious and more subtle. Hallowe'en, the Celtic Samhain and the Christian All Souls' Day, falls on 31 October. That pretty much marks the end of the apple harvest and thus there would always have been a surfeit of apples with which to mark the occasion. 'Bobbing (or Dooking) for Apples' was a traditional Hallowe'en game for the children who dressed up and went from house to house, performing simple acts for a reward. In Scotland, this is called guising – the children were 'disguised' by their costumes. (There was no necessity for the guises to be skeletons, were-wolves, ghosts or witches, or anything scary. Our son, who hated being made to dress up with a vengeance, would only go to the village Hallowe'en party as a forester, carrying his dad's chainsaw. Perhaps that was scary enough!) To get their sweeties, or sometimes just for fun, children had to retrieve apples from a bowl of water using only their teeth. A variation on this is stringing apples up from a line and making partygoers eat them without using their hands.

If there were plenty of apples so that you could afford to let some get bruised, you could line up two teams of children – or adults – and give the ones at the front of each line an apple, which had to be passed down the line to the end. Whichever team got its apple home first won – but with hands tied behind backs!

Tricky – but none of this 'trick or treat' commercialism, which has swamped the traditional Hallowe'en for many. Hallowe'en, with or without ghosts, should be a fun experience for guisers and householders alike. But a little of the supernatural lurks just around the corner ... a common game to get children to compete for the longest unbroken peeling of an apple is followed by throwing the peel over their shoulders. The letter closest to the shape of the peel on the ground magically foretells the initial of the person they would marry.

And the other explanation for apple consumption at this festival (whether plain or coated in toffee) is that apples were sacred to the Celtic peoples, who knew this time as Samhain, that is, the doorway between light and summer and the darkness of winter. Apples were eaten to encourage only good spirits to cross through the thin veil separating their world from ours at this time of change.

## Chapter Ten

# Orchard Pests and How to Confound Them

We have mentioned the uninvited guests (pests!) to the orchard and diseases quite a bit now, from the dangers of pruning at the wrong time to the need to install tree protection right from planting day. This chapter and the next look at some of the culprits and the damage they can cause in more detail.

## Invertebrates

'Invertebrate' covers molluscs (snails and slugs), insects, arachnids (spiders and relatives) and all other 'creepy crawlies' with a hard exoskeleton rather than a backbone. If they cause physical damage, this may be the tip of an iceberg, as many invertebrates – especially aphids – are vectors for diseases, to be covered in Chapter 11, or can lead to other serious problems. Often the first sign of pest damage, however, is holes appearing in leaves, or messy stuff in the forks of twigs. It is really hard to catch invertebrates 'in the act', because either they have already been and gone (in which case maybe there isn't a problem), or they are too well hidden and camouflaged. Some are just too small to be seen with the naked eye. And if a few holes from a departed invertebrate are all you observe, we would advise you not to worry unduly.

This section is ordered according to where the damage is seen on the tree. Ways to prevent or remove the pest/guest invasion by physical and biological control are discussed, but we are not going to recommend life-destroying chemicals or routine 'preventative' spraying. The reasons for this are given above

and in our concluding chapter, 'A Holistic Orchard'. Non-harmful pest-specific options, however, will be considered.

## Invertebrate damage to leaves

Holes, tears and abrasions on fruit-tree leaves may appear for a wide variety of reasons. A clumsy blackbird may have accidentally landed on a fragile new leaf. The dog may have taken a nibble, or a leafcutter bee may have cut out some perfect circles for nest building. Obviously, no problems there. Other holes may be the result, not of anything eating or tearing the leaf, but of a disease, which is more worrying and will be discussed in the next chapter. But some holes *are* down to invertebrates, as are other peculiar things that happen to leaves.

### Aphids and suckers

These are probably the fruit-tree grower's number one invertebrate enemy. The cherry blackfly overwinters in buds and bark of all types of cherry, emerging to start eating as the buds open. Leaves at the ends of shoots are first to be affected, wrinkling up, then curling, and eventually turning black. The distortion is caused because the aphids are sucking the sap out. The blossom is largely destroyed and if you uncurl the leaves, you'll find the little blighters tucked up inside. If they are not, suspect something else. There is hope if you catch them at the first sign and squash the colonies. You can also cut off and destroy affected opening leaves and even shoots, though you may lose some of your fruit crop. It's a big ask to be confident you've got every last one, though, as aphids breed at an immoral rate.

You can also drench the shoots with a soft soap solution. This blocks the breathing holes in the aphid's exoskeleton, causing death. But go under and inside the leaves; it is very difficult to get them all. We never have! Prevention, of course, is better than cure, and if you start to get damage from this aphid, you could consider one of the plant-based 'winter washes', which are sprayed on to the tree and which kill the overwintering eggs. (Tar oil, which killed everything in sight, is thankfully no longer available due to carcinogens in the mix.)

Other aphids to look out for are the rosy apple aphid and the rosy leaf-curling aphids, which cause major foliage damage and, in the case of the former, stunted fruit growth. Then there are the aphid-like relatives, the suckers. The apple sucker always starts its work in the blossom and moves on seamlessly to the leaves, having wiped out any chance of fruit forming. The pear sucker overwinters as an adult so is less susceptible to a winter wash, but fortunately isn't that common.

All aphids suck sap from the tree and sap is a sugary substance. When it passes through the digestive system of your average aphid, the sugars are more concentrated, leading to black patches of sooty mould colonising the foliage. If you see sooty mould, there are aphids hiding somewhere; meanwhile the sooty

Aphids can make a real mess of cherry shoots.

These black aphids are the culprit on cherry.

mould is blocking out light and clogging pores, with the result that the tree's ability to photosynthesise is severely compromised.

## Spider mites

The voracious fruit-tree red spider mite does not leave holes, or, at least, not ones that are big enough to see. What you will notice is the foliage on affected trees becoming dull and 'peely-wally', which is Scots for pale, yellowish-grey and sickly looking. Fruit-tree red spider mites are very, very small, eight-legged and yes, red … but if you think you see one *do not squash it*! The ones you can see with the naked eye are actually a wonderful predatory mite, working away with other predators on your behalf at controlling any infestation. You would need very good eyesight to see individual fruit-tree red spider mites without a decent hand lens. The predators also move pretty fast, whereas the pests slouch around – so you can be sure if you see one scurrying it's a predator in pursuit of dinner.

We have never seen the fruit-tree red spider mite causing problems on our outdoor trees, but we do have them on the peach tree that lives in a greenhouse. They thrive in dry, warm conditions, so regularly spraying the hose on tree, floor and glass is sufficient control for us. You can, however, buy the predatory mite *Phytoseiulus* for glasshouse use if things get serious.

Aphids on apple leaves.

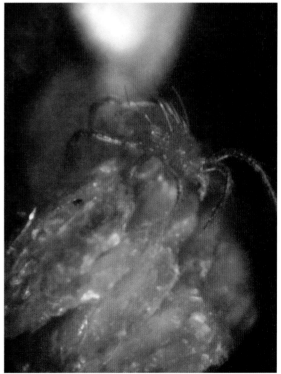

*Phytoseiulus persimilis* is a predatory mite. It loves glasshouse red spider mites for dinner. (Wikimedia Commons)

Signs of fruit-tree red spider mite feeding on peach leaves.

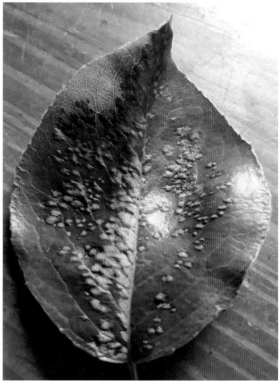

Early symptoms of pear blister mite.

## Leaf miners, gall mites and blister mites

Many small insects burrow (or eggs are laid) into the leaf itself, which actually consists of two layers, called laminae. Here is a cosy home for the apple leaf miner, which is the larva of a tiny moth. It crawls around eating the inside of the leaf and making interesting tunnels and, when ready to emerge as an adult, eats its way out. However, there is no need to panic about this leaf miner, as, by the time it's in the leaf, the season is usually wearing on and no harm is done to the fruit crop. The apple tree will put out new leaves next year anyway. You may even get to like your artistic little squatters!

The plum leaf gall mite is similarly harmless. It sucks away at sap from the underside of the plum leaf in spring, then secretes chemicals that create whitish bumps, or galls, on the upper side. Damsons and plums are also susceptible.

Blister mite damage can look truly alarming, but the harm done is relatively small. The pear leaf blister is caused by a microscopic gall mite living inside the leaves. As they feed, they secrete chemicals that cause pinkish or yellowish blisters to puff up on either side of the leaf midrib.

## Sawflies and capsid bugs

Sawflies are insects whose caterpillars feed voraciously on the leaves of certain plants. They are often specific to a certain genus or species. There is one whose target plants are pear and cherry trees, plus a few others in the same family. The pear and cherry slugworm is well-named – the larvae exude a black slime and look like small, black slugs. They are difficult to mistake, easy to see, but difficult to control except by picking them off.

The pear slugworm munches away at leaves.

Capsid bugs are also insects, but they may produce two generations every year and each generation may have different feeding habits. The apple capsid feeds on foliage to begin with, so you may find them among chewed and distorted young leaves towards the ends of fruiting spurs. The brown feeding trails on the leaves are a telltale sign. Then they move on to fruit, so we'll return to them later.

## Invertebrate damage to stems, twigs, bark and branch

### Woolly aphids

Woolly aphids deserve special attention. Although they are often spotted in the leaf axils, they actually feed on sap from young stems and twigs. As they go on their merry way devouring your apple tree, they secrete a dense, dirty white woolly substance, which eventually rings alarm bells to the orchardist. Needless to say, by then they are hard to get rid of. You can find them tucked into cracks in the bark, pruning cuts and indeed any little crevice. If caught

in spring, they will have done little damage. At this time, the naked aphids are wingless, hiding in their woolly protection without spreading too far. But in summer, when there are plenty of young sappy shoots to sustain them, a winged generation appears and the damage levels ramp up, eventually making fruit picking a sticky and unpleasant task.

How can woolly aphids be controlled? Catching them early and dabbing them with a big paintbrush dipped in soapy water can help. That could, however,

Woolly aphid damage on an apple.

become an unending task if your trees are large. There is a biological control – the tiny *Aphelinus* wasp, which parasitises the aphids by laying its eggs in them. However, all aphids have an abundance of natural predators that can, and should, be encouraged to reside in your fruit garden. Ladybirds, lacewings and hoverflies are among the best known, but never discount small birds, especially of the titmouse family, in their insect-eating phase. And you can take heart that, because of all the woolly effusion, the actual damage is less than it seems.

## Moth larvae

One of the most alarming sights on fruit trees – and one that makes most of us want to run away from rather than tackle – is that of twigs, leaves and branches getting meshed up together by what look like a swarm of sticky cobwebs. The damage here is caused by the larvae of one of a number of small, inoffensive-looking moths. The 'looper' caterpillars of the winter moth are the least alarming, as by and large they stick to making holes and 'stitching up' leaves into small cigar-like rolls with their webs, then skulking in them. Winter moths are one of the species in which the female is wingless. To get into the tree, lay her eggs and raise a brood that will create round, corky scars on new leaves, blossom and developing fruit, she has to climb up the trunk, So, ringing the trunk with a grease band of something sticky but non-toxic should foil her plans.

Lackey and brown-tail moths are the ones that make cobwebby tents. They are most likely to do this on hawthorn or blackthorn in the hedgerow, but if your orchard is bounded by these shrubs, the moths will often migrate to your apple trees in an infested year. It's one of the reasons why hawthorn in particular is not recommended for orchard shelter belts. Lackey moths can be readily controlled if you suspect they are around – look for the eggs that they conveniently lay in rings around stems. These can be easily destroyed and, once again, natural predators will help you out.

Caterpillars of a number of species can destroy leaves and shoots in summer.

Typical winter moth caterpillar damage to leaves.

Tents erected by moth larvae.

## Scale insects

There are several scale insects that can infest fruit trees. Like aphids, they are sucking insects that excrete honeydew. The mussel scale is found on the bark of apple trees where, after a few days of crawling around as newly hatched wanderers occasionally feeding on the fruit, they settle in large numbers. This suffocation by scale insect, as well as the secondary disease problems caused by honeydew, makes it a pest; one that is hard to spot. Oyster scale is rounder and less prolific in its breeding, as is the pear scale mite. Mussel scales are most likely to be found on old, neglected trees, especially where they have migrated into the garden from nearby hawthorn. Good tree care and avoidance of hawthorn in the hedge are sensible preventative measures, but if you are unlucky enough to inherit a severe infestation, a plant-based

winter wash may be needed to prevent trees becoming seriously debilitated.

One more pest of the wood and branches of fruit trees (among many others) to consider is the beautiful, large, black and white leopard moth, which lays its eggs on the tree. The caterpillars eat their way into the wood and pupate under the bark. It's not seen much, if at all, north of Yorkshire, but we would love to find one. We read that they can be a real problem for olive farmers, so maybe with climate change we should be aware of this splendid beast.

## Invertebrate damage to blossom and fruit

### Capsid bugs

Blossom and fruit pests go together – if something starts on fruit-tree blossom, it will probably have a serious detrimental effect on fruit. Some pests, on the other hand, make a beeline for the fruit as it ripens, which is also when some of those leaf and stem pests switch their attention to something sweeter. For example, after munching on foliage, the apple capsid bug then feeds on the apples. While this is not particularly damaging in itself, it causes a reaction in the fruit that leaves an irregular, raised, corky scar. Cut it off and the rest of the apple will still be delicious.

### Moth larvae

Winter moths will infest blossom as well as leaves on fruit trees, moving seamlessly on to the fruit, but usually only causing superficial damage as described above. Much more alarming are the effects of a really big winter moth population, which can completely defoliate a tree. But by the midsummer most of the caterpillars will have pupated in the soil – you might see them descending on silken threads individually – and, fortunately, the leaves regrow.

Capsid bug damage on an apple.

Another group of the cobweb-making moths targets developing fruit – the tortrix family. The fruitlet-mining tortrix is given away by the telltale webbing sealing up the space between developing apples or plums. Within this enclosure, the larvae – recognisable by their white bodies and black heads – nibble away at the fruit surface, leaving small holes or scars. The fruitlet-mining tortrix's attention is diverted from leaves to fruits in summer and the larvae are more yellowish-green in colour. The plum fruit moth larva is a pinkish colour and burrows into the very heart of the fruit, making it uneatable. As affected plums ripen prematurely, some control can be had by picking them off and destroying them before the larvae leave to pupate in the tree's bark.

The use of pheromone traps was encouraged primarily among commercial growers to estimate the population size of the given pest and inform the best time for spraying. Basically, pheromone traps attract the males of the pest species. In some cases, such as the plum fruit moth, they can interfere with mating sufficiently to provide some control.

Pheromone traps are also available for the dreaded codling moth, which enters developing apples and pears, burrows through to the core, makes a heck of a mess filling itself up as the fruit develops, then leaves to pupate under the bark. Apart from luring the males away with the traps, good orchard hygiene is crucial to reducing the size of an attack – never leave prunings or damaged fruit lying around under the tree for the pupae to emerge as adult moths.

## Weevils

Apple blossom weevils target blossom on both apples and pears, causing a brown capping to develop on the blossom cluster, which prevents fruit from forming. As these weevils hibernate in rough bark, it is possible to trap (and remove) them in the hibernating stage by wrapping rough sacking round the tree if you suspect their presence. They will readily go to sleep in that if there are no other options.

Pheromone trap being used to control codling moth.

Apple weevils can reduce successful pollination.

The ribbon scar of apple sawfly.

Do not become alarmed if flocks of blue or coal tits appear to be eating your fruit blossom. They are actually ferreting out blossom weevils, aphids and other unsavoury characters.

## Pear midge

The pear midge is a tiny insect that lays eggs in developing fruit. The larvae cause the little pear first to grow unnaturally round, rather than pear-shaped, then to discolour, before finally turning black. If you are observant, you can learn to spot the affected fruit. Remove and destroy them. Don't let them fall on the ground and stay there – the larvae will only pupate, to emerge and start the cycle again next year.

## Apple sawfly

A final menace to blossom and fruit is the rather interesting apple sawfly. It lays its eggs in the blossom and when the fruit starts to grow, the white-bodied, black-headed larvae burrow under its skin and typically make a 'C'-shaped ribbon scar from eye to centre, before delving down to the core. As the scar is so diagnostic, it's easy to spot and remove affected fruit.

There are other invertebrate pests; indeed, you could fill a book with them and of course people have. We have described the ones most likely to cause a problem, plus a few interesting enough to be aware of. It's so easy to assume that every little creature is a disaster, but some are scarcely more than an irritant, or may even be beneficial. Think about what you regard as an acceptable level of damage. It's strange how when buying fruit from the supermarket, we check for – and reject – those with markings or deformities, but when picking the fruit from your own tree, you will not be put off by the odd corky scar or bird peck that you can just cut out. You may even cut away the undamaged bits of apple round the codling moth larva and eat them if it's your favourite variety – it certainly happens in this house! If you plan to sell your fruit, you will have different standards, of course, and that's why having an awareness of troublesome organisms is essential.

## Vertebrates

### Deer

Several wild mammals can cause considerable damage to fruit trees. Deer of all species plus hybrids will happily munch the leafy tips of trees and at various times scrape the trunk with their antlers to mark territory. Roe deer are particularly problematic, especially where an orchard borders a woodland, as they will chew on branches at dawn and dusk. The answer is to guard your trees to at least 1.5m (5ft), either just the trunk, or with a wider net and post structure that will protect some of the upper branches also. As discussed in Chapter 4, sometimes the best option is to put a deer fence around the entire orchard, taking care to make the gate deer-proof as well.

## Rabbits

Rabbits will eat the soft bark of young trees at the base, but especially scrape and eat the bark of mature trees when the ground is frozen and they can't get at their usual forage. Such damage can be 50–80cm (20–32in) high if there is deep snow on the ground. Use spiral guards on all trees to 45cm (18in), making sure that they are pushed down into the ground. Rabbit-netting around the base, or enclosing the whole orchard in a rabbit-proof fence that folds under the turf to prevent them from burrowing under, is worth

Deer damage to young stems can be catastrophic.

doing in larger orchards. Again, pay attention to the gate, as it will need to be rabbit-proof at and below ground, too.

If there are a lot of rabbits in your site, then consider eradicating them before planting a new orchard, as you will inevitably have problems. They like to hide in old sheds and abandoned cars, so make sure in rabbit country that your orchard is not full of these 'sanctuaries'. Hares can also be very damaging to trees, but generally prefer more open ground in which to hide.

## Voles

Voles can cause catastrophic damage to the roots of trees, as well as grazing their bases, again especially in frosty conditions. Vole numbers fluctuate, but if you leave too much long grass around your trees, they will

Roe deer raid the orchard in winter.

not be controlled by natural predators such as owls, which can hunt successfully in short meadows, but cannot catch their prey in tangled long grass. Where foxes are routinely killed, note that the vole population will be high as a result. Give your grass a final mow in November or even December to deter voles from scuttling across this no-man's land.

If you put your trees in tree shelters, you might find that voles move in too and make a nest at the base. It is worth checking for that problem in winter. Also lift and check under mulch mats for vole runs or tunnels. Serious outbreaks may necessitate trapping and relocating them. Encourage kestrels to patrol the orchard by putting up nest boxes and tall posts, or, if all else fails, borrow a (well-trained) terrier from a friend!

by blue tits and similar birds is only because they are searching out insects – including the aforementioned aphids and caterpillars – and the benefit far outweighs the odd pecked flower cluster.

Various birds do peck at ripening fruits. Sometimes, you just have to get up earlier. To any wildlife enthusiast, this is just fair game and not a problem – except when wasps follow behind them, attracted by the first sniff of rot and fermentation. Plums are the most susceptible and after a wasp attack, the fruit is ruined for storage or sale, quite apart from the risks involved in harvest. Just be aware and remove damaged fruit when seen, if you can, before the wasps arrive, while keeping in mind the good pollination and pest-control services wasps do the rest of the year.

## Birds

Bullfinches eat buds. Exactly how damaging they are is open to debate, as there should be plenty of buds remaining after bullfinches have moved through an orchard. Andrew chases them off his best trees, but they are one of our favourite birds, so Margaret invites them back. We've never had a fruit shortage that could be laid at the door of the bullfinch, but some friends insist they have. Any damage caused

## Livestock

Despite several references to having sheep in orchards, it is definitely not something we would encourage. Herbivores and fruit trees do not go together. Sheep will stand up on their hind legs and chew at branches higher up in the tree. They will also strip bark. Some old trees on vigorous stocks may cope with this, such as in the farm cider orchards of Devon. These well-established orchards with healthy, tall trees may be

Voles escape predators in the long grass and come out to eat trees.

The bullfinch – too handsome to be called a pest.

Beaver activity is unmissable, so don't plant orchard trees near a beaver watercourse.

suitable for recently turned-out young lambs to graze, but your shiny new orchard is not! An experiment in Northern Ireland put sheep in a modern orchard within a mobile electric fence.[10] This had to be moved regularly, because if the sheep ran out of grass they very quickly started on the trees.

Cattle also like to forage foliage and love pears. This is something we've witnessed in the old Carse of Gowrie orchards. Cows will also lean against old trees and push them over. Sheep, cattle and horses all use trees as rubbing posts, fraying the bark and damaging the stability of the trunk. Dogs, cats and badgers may also scratch the bark to keep their claws in good condition. Wrapping some chicken netting around trunks can help to protect them.

A fairly recent consideration here in Scotland – and soon across Britain – is beaver damage. They love apple trees! The signs that beavers are engaged in serious tree-food farming or hydrology are unmistakeable. If you are lucky enough to live in beaver country, enjoy them – but you might want to avoid siting your orchard too close to the river or burn.

When trees are wall-trained, especially on old walls, occasionally buds and bark are chewed mysteriously high up in the branches. This is likely to be mice or rats living in wall crevices or an abandoned bothy behind the wall. We have probably said enough about the worst mammalian orchard pest – the human with a mower or strimmer – in Chapter 4, so will not return there!

Damage to the stem low down on the tree could be from voles, or a strimmer.

# The mysteries of mistletoe

Pest, poisonous parasite, or a privilege to have in your orchard? Mistletoe is a strange and, to many, mysterious plant. It was sacred in the time of the druids and known as the Golden Bough. It is semi-parasitic on its host tree, where it grows slowly, taking water and nutrients from the tree and eventually forming a huge ball of pale, evergreen foliage and the familiar, translucent white berries. Despite druidic rumours, mistletoe on oak trees is actually very unusual in Britain. It prefers to grow on members of the poplar family ... and on apple trees.

Although poisonous to humans, despite having some medicinal properties, the berries of mistletoe are much sought after by certain birds (such as the mistle thrush) and are spread from tree to tree by the birds wiping their beaks on the bark. The tiny seeds sit for a couple of years doing very little beyond taking hold, but then the plant begins to grow. Mistletoe thrives in the large commercial orchards of Hereford and Worcester. Although it rarely kills its host, a strong crop of mistletoe will weaken a tree and cause it to be less productive. The fruit growers and cider-makers control mistletoe by making a lucrative second income from it around Christmas time! Luckily for the mistletoe, our adherence to ancient customs means eradication is not on the agenda.

Mistletoe has always been associated with magic and fertility, which may be the reason why kissing under the mistletoe is such a deeply embedded pagan tradition inserted into the Christian festival of Christmas.

Magical mistletoe.

## Chapter Eleven

# Orchard Diseases and Disorders

## What is the difference between a disease and a disorder?

A disease, whether affecting an animal, such as a human, or a plant, such as a cherry tree, is caused by an alien organism entering the body of the one affected – that is, they are not only *affected*, but also *infected*. Most disease organisms (certainly the ones we are concerned with in this book) are one of the following three types:

- a fungus
- a bacterium
- a virus

When your tree is infected, it will show symptoms; signs that everything isn't quite right. However, fruit trees often display very clear signs that something is wrong, without having a causative disease organism involved at all.

For example, when the edges of newly unfurled pear leaves go brown, dry and shrivelled, it may be due to frost damage and not one of the pests and diseases that can cause the same thing to happen. The apple tree with poor, wishy-washy, yellowing foliage and unimpressive growth may look like that because there isn't enough nitrogen in the soil, rather than because of a red spider mite attack. The plum tree that never bears fruit may be perfectly healthy, but someone's not pruning it correctly. All these are examples of disorders.

It gets complicated when pests, diseases and disorders interact, as is very often the case. The tree starved of nutrients is more likely to succumb to an attack of fungal or bacterial disease. Aphids carry viral diseases and spread them from tree to tree. Severe frosts can crack the bark of an apple tree and invite in the spores of fungal canker – but so can an untreated colony of woolly aphids. All these, and many other interactions, need to be considered when you are faced with a poorly tree. Let's therefore look at the main tree diseases in turn.

## Fungal diseases

### Apple and pear scab

Scab mostly exhibits itself on fruit skin as small round brown patches. It is not usually a problem when using the mature fruit domestically, but can be a problem if severe, or if you are selling commercially. Often, it's only on the skin and the peeled apple is usable, but try telling that to the customer!

Apple scab is prevalent in high rainfall areas of the UK.

What you may not realise is that scab has likely infected the fruit from the leaves. Leaves will have yellow patches with a brown edge, or brown irregular circles on the surface, and the spores splash on to the young fruit as they develop. When the leaves drop in the autumn they often have not rotted down by the following spring (especially with climate change and warmer winters) and can reinfect the new leaves, twigs and fruit. Some varieties are very susceptible, others less so, but none are immune to this disease, despite what some catalogues say. If you have a tree that has got so bad that its fruit are unusable, pull it out and plant a different variety.

To break the cycle, remove the leaves that fall on to the ground in the autumn, either by raking them up, or running them over with a mower and collecting box. Pick off any remaining dead fruit (and leaves) hanging on the tree. Prune the tree regularly to get a succession of new healthy branches each year. Cut out any twigs that have splits in the bark, discoloured twigs, or twigs with large dark spots, as these may all be a sign of scab or canker.

Professional growers frequently spray the leaves with a protective fungicide in order to prevent the spores blowing in. Growing your apples in open and sunny positions in the garden and away from the dampness and drip line under trees will help enormously, as spraying is not a feasible cure for gardeners. Orchards in the wetter west will be more susceptible than the dryer east of the British Isles, but don't generalise. The east side of a hill in Wales may be drier than an open fen in the Midlands. Look to your local microclimate rather than average rainfall statistics. Varieties said to have some resistance to scab are listed in Table 6.

Pear scab is quite common and results in sunken dark cracks and spots along all the twigs. It severely restricts the growth and health of infected trees. Neglected trees are often affected, as well as those shaded next to big trees. Regular pruning and removal of severely infected trees is the best way to keep the rest of your trees healthy. Take off moribund, desiccated fruit and rake up debris, leaves and twigs, disposing of them in your municipal compost bin. (Municipal composting should reach the higher temperatures you won't get in most domestic heaps, which are enough to destroy the disease organisms.) Prune hard to get the trees growing healthy young shoots.

### Table 6: Apple and pear varieties with some resistance to scab

| Apples | Pears |
| --- | --- |
| Adam's Pearmain | Beurre Hardy |
| Ashmead's Kernel | Black Worcester |
| Beauty of Bath | Catillac |
| Discovery | Gorham |
| Edward VII | Hessle |
| Exeter Cross | Jargonelle |
| Grenadier | |
| King of the Pippins | |
| Lord Derby | |
| Miller's Seedling | |
| Monarch | |
| Red Devil | |
| Reverend W. Wilkes | |
| Rosemary Russet | |
| Stirling Castle | |
| Winston | |

Scab on pear twigs can severely weaken the trees.

## Apple and pear canker

This is much more serious. It is a fungal disease producing tiny red fruiting bodies that can blow in the wind in cool, wet weather to other trees and infect damaged bark and twigs. Over the winter, you may see these fruiting bodies around a wound a year after infection if you look closely. If you do spot it, it's best immediately to cut around these wounds to healthy wood. The fungus destroys bits of bark and cambium, and can eventually girdle a whole branch or twig, thus killing everything above the wound site. Cutting canker out is quite a tricky operation, requiring a good knife – it is not usually possible to get in with secateurs.

Always look for cankered shoots first when pruning and remove them. Look for flaking or cracked bark, sometimes girdling a whole shoot and causing its top to die. Sunken areas of bark are another symptom. Dispose of the pruned cankered twigs, as the fungi will still be live and spreading spores for a while. If you have inherited a mildly infected tree and prune out the damaged shoots, you may be able to live with it, as long as the fruit production is good and you can't see live fungal bodies.

However, heavily infected older trees may have more dieback than can be realistically pruned out each year and would be impossible to clean up. Likewise, if your tree has been girdled around the main stem, the only course of action is to replace it in order to protect neighbouring trees, to which it may be passing fungal spores (see Chapter 9). Fungal diseases proliferate in crowded, damp, dark parts of the tree, so by pruning to allow light and air around the twigs and not creating damp corners, you can generally avoid too much infection.

Canker is often associated with woolly aphid lesions, although which causes which is open to debate. Canker seems to be rarer on pears, although pruning out dangerous live lesions from pear scab is the best course of prevention. Remember to inspect your shelter belts and nearby old woodland for cankered wood that also might be a source of the disease. Look for signs of coral spot fungus, which indicates dead wood.

## Powdery mildew

Mildew is another fungal disease, exhibiting as a white powdery coating on the first new leaves, that

Twig canker can be pruned out.

is, on the cluster of leaves on the tip of the shoots in spring. It can set the tree's growth and general health back, so best to grab a handful of these leaves as you are passing and dispose of them in your municipal composting bin, or burn well away from the orchard.

Reportedly, powdery mildew is bad in dry, warm periods and climates, but we have noticed it in wet springs, too. Keeping soil moisture levels up is important and this is readily achieved by using an annual mulch of organic matter. It is also reported that summer applications of seaweed are effective in preventing this disease. Crucial, however, is the need to break the infection cycle (the fungus overwinters on the tree to reinfect foliage and blossom in spring), so be vigilant about removing affected shoots. It is usually easy to keep it under control by this method. Commercial growers use applications of organically approved sulphur as a fungicide when the flower buds are at pink bud stage.

## Silverleaf

Silverleaf can be very serious and infects many thousands of plum trees. It is also found to affect cherries and, occasionally, apples. It is fungal and spreads from tree to tree in warm, wet weather from small fungal brackets (*Chondrostereum purpureum*) growing in tall tiers on dead stumps and branches from a wide variety of trees and shrubs. It is very aptly named, as the main symptom is a silvery colour on the upper side of leaves. Often one branch at a time dies off each year. When cut, the wood will show a foxy-brown stain. Make sure that you remove the branch to at least 15cm (6in) below the last spotted staining of the wood. If affected branches are not removed in this way, then the whole tree will eventually die.

The brackets are very common in woods and in neglected plum orchards, so don't leave your old plum trees to hang around beyond their useful life in your orchard. Make sure that any dead stumps or diseased wood from plum trees are taken away.

Prevention is the only sensible cause of action, as it is safe to assume that the spores will be in the atmosphere on calm, moist days after rain, especially in autumn and early winter. They will readily enter any pruning wound and this is one reason we only prune plum trees in summer, or at the very least in growth, when the wounds can heal quickly. Choose a dry, calm period. Often there will be fruit on the tree at the time, or you can prune immediately after harvest. Make sure that your pruning tools are clean and sterilise them using methylated spirit or similar, before moving on to the next tree. We don't usually

Mildew on apple shoots can restrict growth.

Silvering of the leaves can be followed by fungi on the branches.

recommend painting pruning wounds, but it can help in this instance, as long as the wound paint is applied straight away. Don't wait until you've pruned the entire plum orchard, as then you will most likely have sealed the fungal spores in rather than out.

Victoria plums are particularly vulnerable and, if not pruned, will often break branches due to fruit weight, thus opening up large wounds for spores to enter. Above all, it is crucial to formative-prune your trees whilst they are young, so that you don't have to carry out a large amount of potentially damaging corrective action later on.

This diesease can, however, be confused with 'false silverleaf', caused by a lack of water or nutrients, so don't jump to conclusions too quickly. If the trees have 'false silverleaf', there will be *no* staining of the wood on affected branches, so do check this important diagnostic feature before panicking.

## Honey fungus

Honey fungus is the name given to a group of fungi (*Armillaria* species), which produce sweet-smelling, delicious-tasting, honey-brown edible mushrooms in autumn. It is now accepted that the many slightly varying mushrooms in this group are in fact different species and not all of them are equally damaging. Some are saprophytic, which means they only live on dead wood and therefore will not infect living trees. However, it may be hard to tell the difference and an invasion of honey fungus in the garden usually causes alarm and fear for the lives of all woody plants therein.

It's not the delectable mushrooms that do the damage, but the formation of fungal threads called rhizomorphs, which travel under the bark of tree roots and, eventually, trunks, at the alarming rate of 1m (39in) a year. Any tree can become infected, but *Malus* and *Prunus* species are certainly susceptible. Trees under stress are much more likely to suffer, with foliage becoming weak and discoloured. Once again, paying attention to the overall health of your trees, with annual mulching, sound nutrition and dealing promptly with damage, will reduce the effects of any attacks. The only way to eliminate the fungus is by removing all stumps and every root. If roots are left in the ground, the fungus can travel along them to find another host tree. This may be a tall order – even impossible.

Although honey fungus is not usually a welcome sight, it's worth noting that we have had it in the garden for over twenty years, appearing in the middle of the lawn presumably from underground roots of long-gone

Honey fungus often starts on old stumps or buried roots.

in very dry conditions. Making sure that your trees are not short of water can help to prevent this, while attending to the overall health of the trees with good pruning, hygiene (like raking up dead and diseased fallen leaves and fruit) and nutrition will all help to avoid fungal shot hole disease.

## Coral spot

Bright orange spots of fungal fruiting bodies are often seen on dead twigs in trees, hedges and shrubs. It is very common. Coral spot (*Nectria cinnabarina*) is largely saprophytic – that is, feeding on dead and decaying wood. However, it can become an issue when a twig dies back (often as a result of canker, *see above*), allowing the fungus to grow down into the live wood below, accelerating dieback. It is easily controlled by pruning it out wherever you see it and removing dead logs on the ground nearby, or any in your old log heap that have it.

trees. We also have a prodigious number of fruit trees, but, touch wood, none has so far been affected by the fungus. Sometimes the mushroom harvest is better than the plum or pear harvest!

## Shot hole

Shot hole is a descriptive symptom. It can indicate a number of things of varying seriousness, but if you see the leaves of a cherry or plum tree starting to look as though they have literally been peppered with shot, look very carefully at the margins of the holes. If they are not ringed with yellow, the cause is probably a fungus. You should also see brown spots on the leaves – this is just an earlier stage in the fungus's development. The brown spots grow into circles, which detach themselves from the rest of the leaf and fall out, leaving the shot holes. Sometimes the causative fungus is powdery mildew, which tends to thrive

## Brown rot

Brown rot (*Botrytis* species) is a very common fungal rot seen in old fruit, which will be familiar to most orchardists. It displays as rings of off-white or pale brown fungal material on the fruit surface,

Coral spot on a dead plum twig.

which turns brown. Remove any damaged old fruits from the tree, as the fungus can also cause brown oval cankers on twigs, especially in wet seasons. If girdled, these twigs will die back. Burn or bury any infected twigs and fruit from the orchard. Hygiene is the key to control. Brown rot will also affect some fruits in store. Get them out before it spreads!

## Blossom wilt

Again, this is a disease well-named because blossom wilt is exactly what you would see, caused by a fungus (*Sclerotinia laxa*), which overwinters on stems as cankers, then moves on to leaves and blossom. It is most frequently seen on plums, pears and cherries, but there is a form that attacks apples, too. It looks like blossom sprays have been frosted, gone brown and shrivelled up. Do ask yourself if there has been a sharp frost! But, if not, there has probably been a spell of damp weather, when the disease spreads most quickly.

Remove these affected shoots and destroy them. If left, the petals can stick to the stems through the greyish mould and cause the infection of ripening fruit, leading to overwintering mummified fruit on the tree. Never leave these mummified fruit either – get rid of them as soon as you spot them. And tidy up fruit lying under the trees to prevent reinfection each year – simple preventative hygiene.

## Peach leaf curl

Peach leaf curl (*Taphrina deformans*) is a fungal disease that can readily be mistaken in the early stages for an infestation of aphids. The leaves typically start to unfurl, then become puckered, twisted and start to blister. When the coloration of the affected leaves turns from pale green to reddish purple and a whitish mould is seen, you are most probably looking at this disease of peaches, nectarines and apricots.

The affected leaves should be removed (they will fall off eventually anyway), which usually gives the tree time to put out a new flush of healthy leaves. Peach leaf curl is most likely to affect outdoor-grown peaches and nectarines, as the fungal spores find their way in during the cold rains from late autumn to early spring. A simple way to prevent this disease is to erect a temporary cover over the tree for the winter – easier said than done, but possible if the tree is wall-trained. As these fruit trees flower very early, the cover may also avoid frost damage as well (but remember pollination!). We grow our peach in an open-doored, unheated greenhouse and this is one disease we've not been troubled with.

Rotten fruit on your trees should be removed.

Peach leaf curl is often seen in trees open to winter rain.

Bacterial canker symptoms include bleeding stems.

## Bacterial diseases

### Bacterial canker

Remember shot hole, that is, the fungal disease that makes holes in the leaves of cherries and other stone fruit, holes with no yellow ring round them? If there are shot-hole symptoms, but the holes are surrounded by yellow haloes, it is most probably bacterial canker, which is much more serious. The symptoms are easy to spot, as is the subsequent dropping of affected leaves, but before this stage is reached, there will be other signs. Flattening and sinking of areas of bark, sometimes girdling twigs and leading to dieback of shoots, will be present. You will also see 'bacterial ooze' emerging from the affected parts of the trunk and branches, collecting like lumps and trickles of orange-coloured resin.

This disease (the organism is one of a couple of species of *Pseudomonas*) is spread during wet spells in spring and autumn, but hardly at all in summer. It is the other main reason for summer-pruning plums and cherries so as to avoid pruning wounds at all other times. It is also very common on garden 'ornamental' cherries (but when is a cherry not ornamental?). So, if you have these nearby, keep an eye on them for symptoms as well. If you feel surrounded by susceptible trees, choose varieties of plum or cherry that have some resistance to bacterial canker, such as Marjorie's Seedling or Warwickshire Drooper (worth it for the name alone!) plums, or Merton Glory cherries. Plum rootstock Pixy is said to be more resistant than St Julien.

It goes without saying that branches affected by bacterial canker need to be removed, well below the point of infection and damage. Sadly, sometimes this means removing the whole tree. Finally, keep an eye on nutrition – cherries and plums that are nitrogen-deficient are much more susceptible. A regular mulching of organic matter will help, but don't 'chuck nitrogen' indiscriminately at your trees either, as this will cause soft, sappy growth that is also very prone to attack – from everything, not just bacterial canker.

## Fireblight

Caused by a bacterium (*Pseudomonas*), this disease can be very serious in orchards. It affects all pome-bearing (apple-like) fruit trees and can occur on a wide range of native trees in the Rosaceae family, too, such as rowans and hawthorns. Often the first symptom is oozing dark sap and then flower death, followed by the shoots dying and wilting at the ends. The way they hang over at the tips of branches resembles a shepherd's crook. Leaves go black and hang on the tree, then cankers may develop on the bark, where the bacterium overwinters. It will eventually kill whole trees. In summer these branches of black leaves are obvious, especially on pears. Scratch beneath the bark of these cankers and you will see the characteristic reddish colouring of infected wood. This will not be seen if you are mistaking the wilting-shoot symptoms of blossom wilt for fireblight – a mistake all too easy to make.

Fireblight is a serious disease, which used to be notifiable right across the country, but it can be arrested in some cases and much can be done to prevent it. First, you can cut out any branches and shoots showing the telltale red colouring below the bark – but you must go 60cm (24in) below the red colouring to stand a chance of getting all the bacteria-infested wood. And this wood must be destroyed by burning, not left lying around. *Erwinia amylovora* will piggyback on pruning tools, in rain-splash and on infected plant material. It used to be uncommon in the north of the country, but is likely to become a bigger issue as the climate warms.

## Crown gall

Crown gall is a disease that affects the roots or crown (base of the trunk or stem) of many woody plants. The culprit is the bacterium *Agrobacterium tumefaciens*, which lives in the soil and infects wounds to this part of the tree. Rapid multiplication causes galls to form, which, if they get out of hand, may impact the flow of water and nutrients from root to branch, causing

Fireblight can cause twig dieback.

dieback. Sometimes, their proliferation makes the tree structurally unstable.

Crown gall is not a very common problem in orchards, but if drainage is impeded and the trees are waterlogged a lot of the year, you may come across it. If you sort out the drainage, crown gall should not occur.

## Viral diseases

### Stony pit virus

This virus affects the flesh of developing pear fruit, causing them to become distorted and knobbly. The stone cells in the flesh die, resulting in patches of dead woody matter that do not make for pleasant eating. Viruses like this often affect only one branch of a tree, therefore you can be pretty sure it's stony pit virus if this is the case. There is no cure, so make sure you don't use wood from affected branches for grafting. (Boron deficiency causes similar symptoms, but affects fruit through the whole of the tree.)

### Plum pox

Plum pox, also known as sharka, is a viral disease transmitted by aphids. It is uncommon in Britain, but can be brought in on plum rootstocks from Europe, hence the rigorous health checks carried out at all commercial nurseries (by DEFRA, administered by SASA (Science & Advice for Scottish Agriculture) in Scotland). Pale yellow-green blotches appear on foliage and the fruit acquire dark brown rings, pitting and other discoloration. They drop early from the tree and do not taste good.

## Disorders

It is hard to separate fruit-tree disorders from diseases, because, as we have seen already in this chapter and the previous one, it is very often a disorder that sets the stage for attack from a pest or disease. And vice-versa – the presence of a pest or disease can make the tree unable to uptake a nutrient, giving it the symptoms of a deficiency, as well as biological

Viruses can cause leaf discoloration but are not always harmful.

attack. The key types of disorder that affect fruit trees are:

- disorders due to nutrient deficiency
- disorders due to environmental factors (weather, drainage, shade, poor pollination and so on)

These types of disorders clearly have no causative organism. To these we would add the many

Frost damage on flowers.

No disease, but an unusual disorder in Britain – sunburn!

The lack of a good stake has allowed this tree to blow over.

Drought symptoms on the leaves of an apple tree.

manifestations of poor health in fruit trees that do have a causative (if unaware) organism:

- poor management by the orchardist.

We can do a great deal, as fruit-tree growers, to protect or correct trees from the first two types of disorder and to prevent the third.

Table 7 shows how some common disorders can be recognised, how they may interact with pests/ diseases and how our actions can either cause or prevent problems arising. As can be seen from this table, while disorders may not always be avoidable, good planning, planting, pruning and nutrition will go a long way towards minimising negative effects.

## Table 7: How fruit-tree disorders interact with diseases, pests and orchard care

| Disorder | How to recognise it | Interactions | Action that can be taken by orchardist |
|---|---|---|---|
| **Nitrogen deficiency** | Poor growth; small leaves; yellow or reddish discoloration to whole leaf; dull appearance | Nutrient deficiencies make fruit trees more susceptible to disease and attack by pests | Ensure regular supplies of nitrogen (which is quickly leached from soils) by mulching with organic matter |
| **Potassium deficiency** | Margins of leaves go brown and look scorched | Associated with poor blossom and fruit production and retention | Regular mulching with potassium-yielding materials such as wood-ash |
| **Magnesium deficiency** | Centre of leaves *between the veins* turn brown | Nutrient deficiencies make fruit trees more susceptible to disease and attack by pests | Seaweed-based feeds help ensure this and other trace elements are available |
| **Iron deficiency** | Yellow discoloration *between the veins* of young leaves | Nutrient deficiencies make fruit trees more susceptible to disease and attack by pests | May be associated with alkaline soils – check soil pH when selecting site |
| **Boron deficiency** | Affects pears – leads to misshapen fruit and brown areas of dead cells in flesh | Can be mistaken for pear stony pit | Apply organic mulch, especially seaweed, to retain easily leached elements |
| **Calcium deficiency** | Causes apple bitter pit – brown spotting and pitting of fruit surface and just below surface | Common where a heavy crop has not been thinned – not enough calcium for all the fruit to develop | Thin heavy crops; conserve soil moisture by mulching to enable uptake of nutrients in dry weather |
| **Waterlogging/ poor drainage** | Unstable tree due to root dieback; bark splits may be seen especially if wetting follows drought | Can cause crown gall | Get the drainage sorted, or avoid planting fruit trees in waterlogged soil |
| **Drought** | Poor growth, leaves small, stunted and fall prematurely; tree fails to thrive and put on growth | Nutrient deficiency accompanies drought, making trees susceptible to pests and diseases | Attend to improvement using organic matter if soil is poor and sandy |
| **Frost damage** | Blossom burned and falls; emerging foliage blistered and cracked; bark may split after severe frost | Bark splits may lead to woolly aphids and other pests and are disease entry points | Avoid planting in frost pockets; attend to nutrition if damage sets tree back |

*(continued)*

| Disorder | How to recognise it | Interactions | Action that can be taken by orchardist |
|---|---|---|---|
| **Gummosis** | Caused by freezing conditions in spring; resin oozes from healthy wood in cherries and plums | Can be mistaken for bacterial canker; creates entry wounds for disease organisms if severe | Ensure trees affected are boosted with balanced feed/mulch in spring |
| **Wind damage** | Various, but pay attention to wind-rocking of young trees destabilising root system and damaging fine roots | Wind at blossom time is a cause of fruit failure and can also affect nutrient uptake if roots affected | Provide shelter belts or windbreak material in exposed situations; be aware of prevailing wind direction; stake trees correctly |
| **Trees do not set fruit** | Many possible causes: frost damage to blossom; lack of pollinators; bad weather at pollination time; lack of suitable polliniser trees; poor pruning | | Plant to encourage pollinators; prune for fruit production |
| **Fruit drop** | Causes include: late frosts; incomplete pollination; drought; poor nutrition; wind. Note that a 'June drop' of excess fruit is normal for most apple trees | | Rake up fallen fruitlets; address water and nutritional needs |

Fruit dropping before it's ripe may be due to wind, drought, or poor nutrition.

# Wassailing

In parts of the country where apples have been traditionally grown, especially for cider, there is a long-standing tradition of wassailing. By rights, this should happen at Twelfth Night – but as wassailing began long before the introduction of the Gregorian calendar, this means 'Old' Twelfth Night, that is, 17 January. With the orchard revival of recent years, most parts of Britain have taken and adapted the tradition to suit their region and the interests of the community. So, the weekend nearest to the seventeenth is fine and any variations are permitted for a joyous event to unfold.

At this time, the apple trees are dormant. Bad spirits need to be driven from the orchard and this is achieved by the wassailers making a huge amount of noise. The firing of shotguns, as was the custom in Herefordshire and the West Country, does not make for good twenty-first century health and safety – but banging loudly on saucepans or drums, shouting or (in Scotland) starting up the bagpipes will all suffice. Traditional wassailing songs will keep everyone happy and warm as they go the rounds of the community orchard, park or village. Some, like the Carhampton Wassail, are ancient; others, among them the Edinburgh Wassail, are modern. It doesn't matter!

Choose the best-producing tree to embody the spirit of the Apple Tree Man. It should be decorated, hung with festive garlands (tartan ribbons go well around here) and pieces of bread or toast soaked in cider for the robin, who is the guardian of the orchard. Toast this 'King Tree' (it can be a Queen if preferred, or a Commoner for republicans) with cider, with song and a lusty WAES HAEL (Good Health). Don't forget to toss some of your cider on to the tree. Thus, the good spirits will come to ensure bushels of apples and plenty of cider the coming year ...

Wassailing got a bit confused with carol-singing over the last century or so. This may be because the traditional ash-wood Wassail Bowl was paraded round a community for the whole twelve days of Christmas and before, so the two became almost synonymous. But never doubt, wassailing has the longer history!

## Chapter Twelve

# The Holistic Orchard

## Getting entangled

You will have noticed that this book has been divided into neat and tidy chapters, each dealing with a different aspect of orchard or fruit-tree management. You may also have noted that we have repeatedly urged holistic orchard care – looking at the whole orchard picture, rather than a series of unconnected aspects. It has been our overarching guiding principle for managing our trees.

Look back at Table 7 at the end of Chapter 11. Notice how so many of the actions we can take to address one issue can either solve, or lead on to, another issue. For example, feeding to address trace element deficiencies will make a tree less susceptible to pest attack. Failure to thin a heavy crop of Hawthornden apples leads to bitter pit due to insufficient calcium (and oh how well we know that one!). These links are everywhere when looking after fruit trees.

Take fungal diseases. You are not going to get far sprinkling athlete's foot (a fungal disease of humans) powder over a fungus-diseased branch on your apple tree. But it *will* help if you select the best site both for and within the orchard for a given tree and don't crowd in too many trees for the space (Chapters 1 and 4). Then choose trees that have some resistance to diseases (for example, scab) that may prevail in your area – local varieties perhaps (Chapter 2), or on disease-resistant rootstocks (Chapter 3). You will help to keep fungal diseases at bay enormously by carrying out excellent formative pruning and training (Chapter 5), and by every successive pruning being carried out at the correct time, using clean tools and

in the best manner (Chapters 7 and 9). Extra fungal disease prevention points are given if you remember the basic orchard hygiene rules of clearing away diseased prunings, fallen leaves, blossom and thinned fruit, all of which can harbour disease (Chapters 6 and 8). If you stay alert to the potential damage that can be caused by certain aphids, suckers and scale insects, you can prevent fungal disease from entering damaged twigs or bark – and keep on top of these pests by encouraging predators, welcoming insects instead of destroying them, adjusting humidity and so on (Chapter 10.)

So, if you have digested the contents of chapters 1 to 10, you scarcely need look at Chapter 11, which is actually 'about' orchard diseases! Except, of course, to note that not all fungi cause disease and that most, usually unseen, are essential to the very existence of trees, plants and life on Earth.

The subject of nutritional deficiencies and disorders, also addressed in Chapter 11, likewise has close links with choosing the right site, taking care of the soil (particularly soil fauna and fungi), planning and spacing, and ensuring that your trees are always in good, healthy condition by feeding and mulching. Mulching feeds the soil, and through it the trees, and is easy to achieve using organic materials. Appropriate and beneficial feeding, as described in chapters 4, 5 and 7, and alluded to in chapters 10 and 11, will give you trees best able to resist the incursions of pests and diseases, shrug off accidental damage and produce good crops.

And those crops? Apples and plums for puddings and pies will not miraculously appear without the major miracle of pollination – which means *you* choosing the right varieties, *you* carrying out pruning and training to get those fruiting spurs and dards developing and *you* creating an orchard that encourages pollinating insects by providing flowers to forage all through the year and places for them to nest, rest or overwinter. Your brilliant, market-worthy crop will be enhanced if you remember to thin excess fruit clusters, harvest the fruit carefully, store the keepers well and drink the juice or cider from the non-keepers along with those pies and puddings!

Really, all of these separate chapters and sets of instructions or suggestions come together in one sentence: Look after the health of your trees, and in so doing, have a care for the health of the planet. The first mind map pictured is to remind you how entangled every aspect of having a healthy and productive orchard is.

## It's not just about the fruit trees

If you are about to start, or are working your way towards, holistic orcharding already, you will soon be thinking: 'This isn't just about having a few fruit trees in the garden.' You don't even need to have the intention – but what you do with your orchard or fruit garden can have so many positive impacts in tackling the environmental crises we face.

You may find, as we have done, that while it's important to be alert to pests and diseases, in an orchard with a balanced ecology, they rarely matter that much. Wildflowers will bring in both the predators who are on your side and pollinators, too. Flowers and tall grasses along the verge of a hedge will create corridors for invertebrate and bird species, with the hedge providing safe roosting and nesting sites, as well as food and shade from the sun. If the hedge is allowed to grow wide at the base and tall, and doesn't get razed half to the ground every year, it will become a star habitat.

You can ensure that other important provisions for wildlife are met, especially as your orchard matures. Water, a pond for amphibians, nest boxes for birds from robins to barn owls, plus bug hotels, if your area lacks hedgerows and dead wood with holes in. And yes, there is an edginess here: we've emphasised

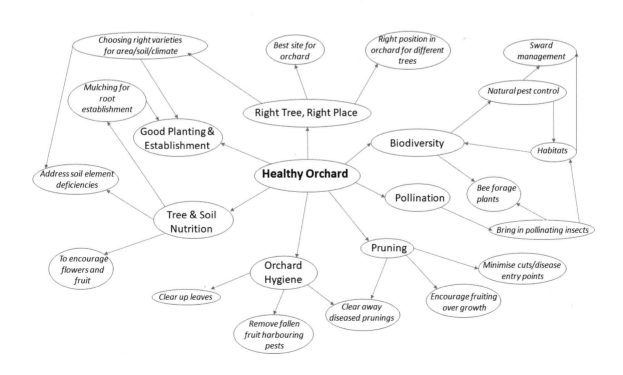

Wildflowers can be left to self-seed under your trees.

A hollow fruit tree is a nest site for birds and spiders.

Water attracts amphibians, essential aids in pest control.

The bark of pear trees can host lichens, mosses and invertebrates.

The fissures in pear bark are home to countless interdependent living creatures.

not to leave dead twigs and rotting fruit all over the place where unwanted organisms can overwinter. But not all dead wood is diseased and as the orchard establishes and ages, it will cope with fallen timber, standing stumps from old dead trees, piles of brushwood for hedgehogs, and even piles of windfalls here and there for fieldfares, blackbirds and badgers.

Certainly, in the early stages, you will have to strike a balance, perhaps having a dedicated spot for the windfalls and a timescale for removal. But, very quickly, your orchard will become an oasis for wildlife – especially the insects and other invertebrates on which we depend, and which have been driven to dangerously low population levels by decades of habitat destruction and insecticide use/abuse.

Orchards, fruit gardens, or a few fruit trees in big pots or against a fence – if managed with love they *will* attract and benefit other living organisms (including you!). They will take in carbon, provide shade, make soil, reduce impacts from flooding. By providing local, affordable, chemical-free food, they can reduce food miles and carbon footprints, as well

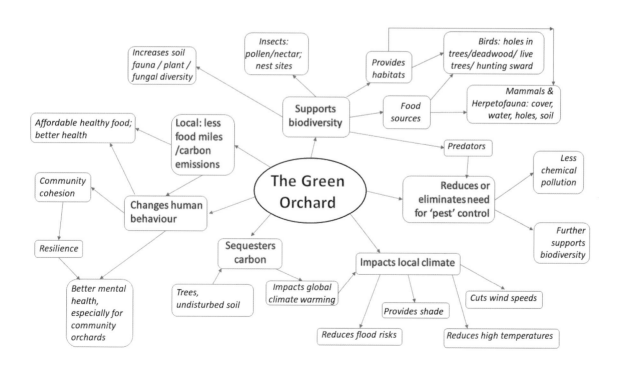

as improving human health. And they just get better and better at all of it. Venerate orchards, for raising the spirits and bringing joy to the soul!

We wish you every success with your orchard project, large or small, wherever and whoever you are. You are part of a very big picture.

A holistic orchard provides for predators like hoverflies to keep aphids under the thumb.

# References

## Chapter 1
[1] The National Orchard Inventory (undertaken by Crispin Hayes Associates in partnership with others, funded by NatureScot) www.orchardrevival.org.uk/inventory-scotland/inventory-report

## Chapter 3
[2] MacDonald, P., *The Manual of Plant Grafting* (Timber Press, 2014)
[3] Garner, R. J., *The Grafter's Handbook* (BAS Printers Ltd, 1979)

## Chapter 5
[4] Morgan, J. & Richards, A., *The New Book of Apples* (Ebury Press, 2002)

## Chapter 6
[5] British Beekeepers' Association www.bbka.org.uk/what-bee-is-this
[6] Baker, H., *RHS Fruit* (Mitchell Beazley, 1980)

## Chapter 7
[7] www.fruitid.com
[8] National Fruit Collection, Brogdale, database: www.nationalfruitcollection.org.uk/search.php

## Chapter 8
[9] Pooley, M. & Lomax, J., *Real Cider Making on a Small Scale* (Nexus Special Interest Ltd, 1999)

## Chapter 10
[10] AGFORWARD www.agforward.eu/grazed-orchards-in-northern-ireland-uk.htm

## On orchard and fruit-tree heritage in Britain

The National Fruit Collection, Brogdale, Kent: www.brogdalecollections.org/the-fruit-collection

Cider Collections: www.nationaltrust.org.uk/news/cider-apple-collection-saved

Perry Pears: www.nationalperrypearcentre.org.uk

Marcher Apple Network: www.marcherapple.net

North Devon traditional orchards: www.orchardslive.org.uk

Gloucestershire: www.glosorchards.org (runs orchard courses)

Northern England: www.northernfruitgroup.com

In Scotland: several local groups including:

- Newburgh Orchard Group in Fife www.newburghorchards.org.uk
- Clyde Valley Orchards Co-operative in Lanarkshire www.clydevalleyorchardscoop.org.uk
- Carse of Gowrie group in Perthshire https://coggweb.wordpress.com

Plant Heritage: promotes National Collections of specified plant species in the UK; thirteen so far dedicated to fruit trees. A National Collection of Malus & Pyrus is held at Megginch Castle, Perthshire; www.plantheritage.org.uk

See heritage orchards and fruit varieties at many National Trust gardens, especially Killerton (www.nationaltrust.org.uk).

National Trust for Scotland properties, including Priorwood and Threave (www.nts.org.uk).

RHS gardens, especially Rosemoor (www.rhs.org.uk), and private gardens and estates open to the public.

*Book*

Copas, L., *A Somerset Pomona – The Cider Apples of Somerset* (Grenadier Publishing, 2001)

## On community orchards and orchard revival

Common Ground: lots of information on traditional orchards and community orchards, in England in particular www.commonground.org.uk

The Orchard Project: creating and celebrating community orchards (UK & Scotland) www.theorchardproject.org.uk

Orchard Revival: as well as the Orchard Inventory (*see* References), promotes orchard revival in Scotland www.orchardrevival.org.uk

SAP (Scottish Apple Producers): https://scottishapples.co.uk

*Book*

Clifford, S. & King, A., *The Apple Source Book* (Hodder & Stoughton, 2007)

## On permaculture and forest gardens

The Permaculture Association: runs courses promoting permaculture design and sustainability in England, Wales and Scotland www.permaculture.org.uk

*Books*

Bell, G., *The Permaculture Way: Practical Steps to Create a Self-sustaining World* (Chelsea Green Publishing, 2005)

Carter, A., *A Food Forest in your Garden* (Permanent Publications, 2021)

Crawford, M., *Creating a Forest Garden: Working with Nature to Grow Edible Crops* (Green Books, 2010)

## On biodiversity and orchards

PTES (People's Trust for Endangered Species) www.ptes.org takes a keen interest in orchard biodiversity.

Biodiversity Partnerships, including Tayside Biodiversity Partnership, often have active programmes to encourage or enhance biodiversity in orchards old and new.

Natural England (www.gov.uk/organisations/natural-england) support traditional orchards, as do NatureScot (www.nature.scot)

*Book*
Macdonald, B. & Gates, N., *Orchard: A Year in England's Eden. An in-depth account of the wildlife of a working traditional Herefordshire orchard* (William Collins, 2020)

## On orchard fruit in the kitchen

Cider presses and equipment: Vigo Presses, Devon, runs courses and supplies quality equipment www.vigopresses.co.uk

The Cider & Perry Academy www.cider-academy.co.uk Training, advice and support from beginner to master level. Based in Gloucestershire.

*Books*
Clifford, S. & King, A., *The Apple Source Book* (Hodder & Stoughton, 2007)
Wörndl, B., *Fruit: Recipes that Celebrate Nature* (Smith Street Books, 2018)

**Abscission** The point for a tree when ethylene levels rise sufficiently to cause it to drop fruit and leaves.

**Biennial bearing** The habit of bearing large crops in alternate years, with little or nothing the year between.

**Chip-budding** A method of grafting using a single bud or 'chip' of your desired tree.

**Dard** A short twig usually ending in a fruit bud.

**Family tree** A tree that has been grafted with several or many varieties.

**Feathered maiden** A one-year old tree that has grown a few branches.

**Fruiting spur** A cluster of buds with the potential to be flower buds.

**Heeling in** Temporarily placing bare-root trees into a trench or pile of compost to protect the roots if there is a delay before planting.

**Lateral branch** Branch coming off the main trunk or a main framework branch.

**Maiden tree** Unbranched one-year-old tree direct from the nursery.

**Pollinator** Insect, animal or other organism that inadvertently transfers pollen from one flower to another when foraging.

**Polliniser** A tree whose pollen is the right type and available at the right time to pollinate another tree to set fruit.

**Russeting** Rusty coating to the skin (usually of an apple), rendering it leathery and good to store.

**Scion** Young twig from a variety for grafting on to rootstock.

**Slow-release (of fertiliser nutrients)** Released and available to trees over an extended period through steady breakdown. Ideal for woody plants.

**Sublateral** Small branch arising from a lateral.

**Top-worked** Tree that has been grafted in the crown, sometimes with more than one variety.